CAYLAN RECOMMENDS

TBN

Family Favorite

R E C I P E S

The Crouch family in December of 1992 from left-to-right:
back row — Paul Jr., Tawny, Jan and Matthew;
front row — Brandon, Brittany, Carra Linda, Paul Sr., Caylan and Laurie.

TBN
P.O. Box A
Santa Ana, California 92711-2101
Prayer Line (714) 731-1000

An Introduction and an Invitation from Gaylan and Jan Crouch

The Invitation has been given! One day SOON, ALL who love Jesus will sit down to a heavenly banquet — the Marriage Supper of the Lamb, and Jesus HIMSELF will serve YOU! This will be the most glorious occasion of celebration for all Believers — can you imagine the dishes that *HE* will serve?

As a little foretaste of that *GLORIOUS DAY*, we have asked many of your favorite evangelists, preachers, ministers and family, representing a beautiful spectrum of diversity in the body of Christ and seen on TBN, to send us their favorite recipes. *Not only* are many different denominations represented here, but many different cultures, too! A little bit of Heaven here on earth! We are family — God's great big beautiful family — and meals bring the family TOGETHER!

Of course, I have included many of my own favorite recipes, and some of our favorite recipes we have collected over the years that we thought you would enjoy having, too! I am sure you will have FUN sitting down to dinner and saying, *"Tonight, I've cooked you Oral Roberts' favorite dinner, Honey!"* Or you may really be adventuresome and prepare one of the exciting *INTERNATIONAL* dishes!

You precious partners, and members, *our family*, who have *Loved*, *Prayed for*, *Watched* and *Supported* Trinity Broadcasting Network through the years - will feel right at HOME with *YOUR* TBN Family's favorite recipes!

To those of you who may be meeting us for the first time, we would like to extend a VERY SPECIAL INVITATION to YOU!

We want to be VERY SURE that *YOU* won't miss Heaven and the most GLORIOUS CELEBRATION SUPPER of all time…the Marriage Supper of the Lamb!

Jesus is ALIVE and He loves *YOU* and wants *you* to be a part of His family, too. If you have never received Him as your personal Savior, we invite you to pray this prayer out loud:

"Dear Jesus, I believe in You. I believe You are the Son of God, that You died for our sins, and that you were buried and rose again according to the scriptures. I'm sorry for the things I've done that hurt You. Forgive me for all my sin. Come into my heart, take charge of my life and make me the way You want me to be. I renounce all sinful practices of the past. Cleanse my heart with Your precious blood. Write my name in Your Book of Life. I confess You now as my Lord and Savior. Fill me with Your Holy Spirit. Thank You, Jesus! In Jesus' name, Amen."

"If you shall confess with your mouth the Lord Jesus, and shall believe in your heart that God has raised Him from the dead, you shall be saved. For with the heart man believes unto righteousness; and with the mouth confession is made unto salvation"

Romans 10:9,10.

If you prayed the prayer of salvation, we would love to hear from you! We would like to send you some literature that will help you grow in faith. Please Write TODAY to:

TBN
P.O. Box A
Santa Ana, CA 92711-2101
or call our Prayer Line at your local TBN station
or (714) 731-1000.

"As God's PARTNERS we beg you not to toss aside this marvelous message of God's great kindness. For God says, 'Your cry came to Me at a favorable time, when the doors of welcome were wide open. I helped you on a day

when Salvation was being offered.' RIGHT NOW God is ready to welcome you. TODAY He is ready to save you"
II Corinthians 6:1,2 *THE LIVING BIBLE.*

Don't put off accepting HIS INVITATION — BE READY!

"...The bridegroom came, and those who were READY went in with Him to the Marriage Feast, and the door was LOCKED"
Matthew 25:10 *THE LIVING BIBLE.*

"Be prepared — all dressed and ready — for your Lord's return from the wedding feast. Then you will be ready to open the door and let Him in the moment He arrives and knocks. There will be great JOY for those who are READY and WAITING for His return. HE HIMSELF will seat them and put on a waiter's uniform and serve them as they sit and eat! He may come at nine o'clock at night - or even at midnight. But whenever He comes there will be joy for His servants who are ready! Everyone would be ready for Him if they knew the exact hour of His return — just as they would be ready for a thief if they knew when he was coming. SO BE READY ALL THE TIME. FOR I, THE MESSIAH, WILL COME WHEN LEAST EXPECTED"
Luke 12:35-40 *THE LIVING BIBLE.*

We love you and Jesus loves you!

"This is Grandma Jan, after eating ALL the recipes in the cookbook."

Love,

Caylan

Table of Contents

Breads

Breads

Date Nut Bread

Recipe from Hazel Crouch
A favorite of Dr. Philip Crouch
Manager Ch. 58, Irving, Texas, and Pastor of
Trinity Christian Center Church of Irving, Texas
Paul Crouch's Brother and Sister-in-law

Pour 1 cup boiling water over dates and butter. Add one teaspoon soda. Cool. Add one beaten egg, sugar, flour sifted with baking powder. Add nuts. Mix well, but do not beat. Bake about one hour. Test with toothpick at 50 minutes (if flat pan used, check after 35 to 40 minutes). Turn out while hot.

1 cup dates, chopped
1 tablespoon butter
1 cup boiling water
1 teaspoon baking soda
1 beaten egg
¾ cup sugar or
    1 cup if used as dessert
1½ cups flour
1 teaspoon baking powder
½ cup chopped nuts

Oven temperature 350°

Bread loaf baking pan

Breads

Charles' Corn Bread

Recipe from Charles and Laurie "Ditty"Quinn
Trinity Agapé Church, Hallandale, Florida
Jan Crouch's Sister and Brother-in-law
A favorite of the Quinn family and many friends

Put skillet in oven to heat thoroughly. Mix all dry ingredients, then add milk, oil, egg and onion. Stir until well blended. Take hot skillet from oven and brush with olive oil thoroughly. Pour mixture in hot skillet and put back into oven. Bake 25 minutes until golden brown. Serve hot.

1 ¼ cups self-rising
    cornmeal
¼ cup self-rising flour
⅛ cup olive oil
1 egg
2 tablespoons sugar
¾ to 1 cup buttermilk
½ to ¾ cup onion,
    finely chopped

Oven temperature 400°

6" Black iron skillet

English Muffin Loaf

Recipe from Janet Paschal
Gospel Recording Artist
Reedsville, North Carolina

Combine 3 cups flour, yeast and sugar. Heat milk and water, low heat. Add to dry mixture and beat well. Stir in remaining flour to make stiff batter. Spoon into loaf pans, greased and sprinkled with cornmeal. Cover and let rise in warm place for 45 minutes. Bake 25 minutes.

2 packages yeast
6 cups self-rising flour
1 tablespoon sugar
2 cups milk
½ cup water
cornmeal

Oven temperature 400°

2 Baking loaf pans
Mixing bowl
Saucepan

Janet's latest album is <u>Simple</u> <u>Trust</u>.

Breads

Oven Baked Puffy Pancakes

Recipe from Ella Smith
A favorite of Pastor Ed Smith
Trinity Christian Center of
Santa Ana, California

Heat oven 425°. Place butter in 13" x 9" baking pan. Place in oven to melt butter. Meanwhile in blender add flour, milk, eggs and salt. Process until smooth. Pour immediately into melted butter. Bake for 20 to 25 minutes. Will puff up, and edges will curl. Cut into wedges and serve with jam, syrup, powdered sugar or fresh fruit.

1 stick butter or
    margarine
1 cup flour
1 cup milk
6 eggs
salt to taste

Oven temperature 425°

13" x 9" Baking pan
Blender or processor

Baked Biscuits

Recipe from Dr. D. James "Jim" and Anne Kennedy
Coral Ridge Presbyterian Church, Fort Lauderdale, Florida
Host of Coral Ridge Hour seen on TBN

Melt oleo or butter in bundt pan. Place Hungry Jack™ Biscuits in the bundt pan on their sides. Bake for 30 minutes.

1 stick oleo or butter
3 cans Hungry Jack™
    Buttermilk Biscuits

Oven temperature 325°

Bundt pan

"I don't have any special recipes for Jim's favorite meal, because he is mostly a 'meat and potatoes' man and everyone knows how to fix those! His favorite meal is rare roast beef, mashed potatoes, and tiny green peas. I wish it were something more exotic!" –Anne

Breads

Wendy's Cinnamon Rolls

Recipe from Casey and Wendy Treat
A favorite of Casey Treat
Christian Faith Center, Seattle, Washington
Host of the Casey Treat program seen on TBN

Put ¼ cup of warm/hot water in a large plastic bowl. Add quick action dry yeast. Sprinkle ¼ cup sugar over yeast, let sit 5 to 10 minutes until foamy and bubbly (discard and start over if yeast does not foam or bubble). Add a couple of the cups of flour along with the one cube butter and mix, using your mixer. Add salt, warm milk and more flour and continuously beat by hand. Add egg and continue to add flour until all flour is used. Dough should be elastic, yet not sticky. Put dough in big pot and cover with a moist towel. Place pot in a pre-warmed 200° oven and turn the oven off. Let rise for one hour or until double is size (time varies by climate). Lightly flour counter and knead dough for several minutes. Roll out dough to ⅓" to ½" thickness. Pat butter over all dough and sprinkle with cinnamon and brown sugar (add optional nuts and/or raisins) to taste. Roll into jelly roll and cut into 1½" to 2" pieces. Place rolls (slightly touching, allowing room for them to rise) in baking pan. Put in pre-warmed 200° oven and turn the oven off. Place a mug of water or a moist towel in the oven, *but not on the rolls.* Let rise ½ hour. Cook at 350° degrees for 12 minutes, then watch until done to your taste.

Frosting:
Beat ingredients until creamy. More milk will create a glaze, less will create a thick frosting. Vary by reducing sugar and substituting 4 to 8 ounces cream cheese.

¼ cup warm/hot water
1 package quick action
    dry yeast
¾ cups lukewarm milk
¼ cup sugar
1 teaspoon salt
two ¼ cubes soft butter
    (room temperature)
3½ to 3¾ cups flour
1 egg (room temperature)
cinnamon
brown sugar
nuts (optional)
raisins (optional)

Frosting:
3 cups powdered sugar
sprinkle of salt
2 to 3 tablespoons butter
1 to 2 teaspoons vanilla
2 tablespoons milk

Rising temperature 200°
Baking temperature 350°

Large plastic bowl
    (warmed with water)
Mixer
Large pot
Large baking pan

Banana Muffins

Recipe from Mrs. Mike (DeAnne) Barber
A favorite of Mike, Brandon, Brittany and Bethany Barber
Mike hosts Proclaim seen on TBN

Cream butter and sugar. Add eggs and bananas. Mix well. Stir in flour and nutmeg. Dissolve baking soda in hot water. Add to banana mixture. Stir in vanilla. Fill greased muffin tins (or paper baking cups) about half full. Bake for 20 minutes or until golden brown.

½ cup butter
1 cup sugar
2 eggs
1 cup mashed bananas
1 ½ cups sifted flour
1 teaspoon nutmeg
1 teaspoon baking soda
2 teaspoons hot water
1 teaspoon vanilla

Oven temperature 350°

Muffin tins
Mixing bowl

Breads

Zucchini Bread

Recipe from Mr. and Mrs. Billy Walker
A favorite of Billy Walker
Country Gospel Singer and Recording Artist
Hendersonville, Tennessee

Mix eggs, oil, sugar, vanilla, flour, baking soda, baking powder, salt and cinnamon. Then add zucchini and nuts. Pour into bundt pan and bake for 1 hour. Let cool in pan 30 minutes. Remove. Finish cooling on wire rack.

3 eggs
1 cup Wesson™ oil
1 ½ cups sugar
3 teaspoons vanilla
3 cups plain flour
1 teaspoon baking soda
¼ teaspoon baking powder
1 teaspoon salt
½ teaspoon cinnamon
1 cup chopped pecans or walnuts
2 cups grated zucchini

Oven temperature 350°

Bundt pan
Mixing bowl

Hot Rolls

Recipe from Bonnie R. Sheaffer
A favorite of Dr. Daniel T. Sheaffer
Crossroads Cathedral, Oklahoma City, Oklahoma
Hosts of The Answer seen on TBN

Mix sugar and salt. Add egg and beat well. Add oil and lukewarm water. Stir well and mix in flour. Put in clean, greased bowl in warm place and let rise until double in bulk. Pour out on floured surface and work down, Then let dough lie for five minutes. Make into rolls. Let rise again, then bake until golden brown.

3 tablespoons sugar
1 teaspoon salt
1 egg
3 tablespoons Wesson™ oil
1 cup lukewarm water
1 package Red Star™
  yeast dissolved in
  ¼ cup warm water
4 cups flour

Oven temperature 400°

Baking tin
Mixing bowl

Breads

Corn Bread Fritters

Recipe from Edith Tripp
A favorite of the LaVerne Tripp family
Gospel Songwriters and Recording Artists
Hosts of The LaVerne Tripp Family program seen on TBN

Mix cornmeal, flour, salt and baking soda. Stir in buttermilk and water until smooth. For thinner fritters increase buttermilk. Drop with spoon into hot skillet. Brown on both sides then serve.

1 cup yellow sifted unbottled cornmeal
1 teaspoon salt
1 cup buttermilk
¾ cup self-rising flour
½ teaspoon baking soda
½ cup water

Skillet

The Tripp's latest album is I'm Still Dancin'.

Wheat Bread

Recipe from Bill and Gloria Gaither
A favorite of Bill Gaither
Gospel Songwriters and Recording Artists
Host of Homeland Harmony seen on TBN

Combine water, sugar, yeast and ginger in a large bowl. Add vegetable oil, honey and condensed milk. Mix together, then add wheat and white flour. Drop batter into two well greased 1 pound or 2 pound coffee cans. Grease plastic lid and seal cans. Let rise until the lid pops off. Then bake in the cans at 330° to 350° for 30 to 40 minutes or until golden brown. Let cool slightly before removing bread from cans. Serve hot.

½ **cup warm water**
1 **teaspoon sugar**
1 **package dry yeast**
⅛ **teaspoon ginger**
2 **teaspoons vegetable oil**
2 **teaspoons honey**
one 15-ounce can condensed
    milk
1 **cup whole wheat flour**
3 **cups unbleached white**
    flour

Oven temperature 330° to 350°

Large Bowl
Electric mixer
Coffee cans with plastic lids

Breads

Old-Time Gingerbread with Warm Lemon Sauce

Recipe from Mrs. Jack (Anna) Hayford
Church on the Way, Van Nuys, California
Dr. Hayford hosts Living Way seen on TBN

Into large bowl, measure ½ cup boiling water and all ingredients (except Warm Lemon Sauce). With mixer at low speed, beat until well blended, constantly scraping bowl with rubber spatula. Increase speed to high, beat 2 minutes, occasionally scraping bowl. Pour batter into pan. Bake 35 to 40 minutes until toothpick inserted in center comes out clean. Cool gingerbread in pan on wire rack 10 minutes to serve warm. Or, cool gingerbread completely on rack to serve later. To serve, prepare Warm Lemon Sauce. Cut gingerbread into 9 squares. Serve with lemon sauce.
Makes 9 servings.

Warm Lemon Sauce:
From 3 large lemons, grate 2 tablespoons, peel and squeeze ¼ cup juice; set aside. In 1 quart saucepan over medium heat, heat 1 cup water, ⅓ cup sugar, and 1 tablespoon cornstarch until mixture boils and thickens slightly, stirring frequently; boil 1 minute. In small bowl, with fork, beat 1 egg yolk; stir in small amount of heated sauce. Slowly pour egg mixture back into sauce, stirring rapidly to prevent lumping. Cook, stirring constantly, until mixture thickens. Remove saucepan from heat. Stir in lemon juice, lemon peel, and 2 tablespoons margarine or butter (¼ stick) until margarine melts.

1¾ cup flour
½ cup sugar
½ cup salad oil
½ cup molasses
1 teaspoon baking soda
1 teaspoon ground ginger
½ teaspoon ground cinnamon
½ teaspoon salt
1 large egg

Warm Lemon Sauce:
3 large lemons (¼ cup juice)
1 cup water
⅓ cup sugar
1 tablespoon cornstarch
1 egg (yolk only)
2 tablespoons margarine or
    butter (¼ stick)

Oven Temperature 350°

9" x 9" Greased and floured pan

"I've enjoyed this since I was a little girl." –Anna

Banana Bread

Recipe from Zonelle Thompson
A favorite of Dwight Thompson
Host of the <u>Dwight Thompson</u> program seen on TBN

In mixer beat 1 egg until light. Add both sugars and butter, mix well. Add mashed bananas. Sift flour and baking soda and fold into batter. Add nuts. Bake in a greased bread pan for 45 minutes.

1½ cups sifted flour
½ cup white sugar
½ cup brown sugar
1 teaspoon baking soda
1 egg
¼ cup melted butter
3 mashed bananas
1 cup chopped walnuts or
**   pecans**
a dash of salt

Oven Temperature 350°

Bread pan
Electric mixer

Breads

Mother Moody's Banana Bread

Recipe from Flora Chastain Moody (not pictured)
A favorite of Flora's grandson, Dr. Jess C. Moody
Shepherd of the Hills Church, Porter Ranch, California
Dr. Moody hosts the Jess Moody program seen on TBN

Cream Crisco™ and sugar. Beat eggs until light and add mashed bananas and lemon juice. Sift flour, soda, and salt together. Add flour mixture to banana mixture. Stir until mixed. Bake in greased loaf pan for 45 to 50 minutes.

⅔ cups Crisco™ (not liquid)
1 cup sugar
2 eggs
1 cup mashed ripe bananas
1 teaspoon lemon juice
2 cups sifted flour
1½ teaspoon soda
½ teaspoon salt

Oven temperature 375°

Loaf pan

Accompaniments

Accompaniments

Fruited Cream Cheese Spread

Recipe from Dotti Casoria
A favorite of John and Dotti Casoria
Bethany Christian Center, Loganville, Georgia
Jan Crouch's Sister and Brother-in-law

Spread almonds in a shallow pan, and bake at 350° for 4 to 5 minutes. Set aside. Place cream cheese on lettuce leaves on a serving tray. Coat the top with chutney, allowing some of the chutney to run off the sides. Sprinkle with toasted almonds. Serve with gingersnaps or wheat crackers.

¼ cup chopped almonds
two 8-ounce packages
cream cheese, softened
lettuce leaves
½ cup mango chutney
or other fruit-flavored
chutney
gingersnaps or
wheat crackers

Oven temperature 350°

Serving tray
Shallow pan

Baked Garlic Spread

Recipe from Cheryl Kartsonakis
A favorite of Dino Kartsonakis
Concert Pianist and Recording Artist

Take 1 whole garlic bulb and cut away top. Place into casserole dish with 1 part water and 12 parts pure olive oil. Bake for 1 hour at 350°. Serve with butter or margarine on hard rolls or French bread.

1 whole garlic bulb
olive oil
butter or margarine
hard rolls or French bread

Oven temperature 350°

Casserole dish

Dino's latest album is <u>Somewhere In Time</u>.

Mexican Relish Dip

Recipe from Mrs. John (Diana) Hagee
A favorite of John Hagee
Cornerstone Church, San Antonio, Texas
Host of Cornerstone and John Hagee Today seen on TBN

Mix all ingredients and add salt to taste. Let sit in refrigerator for 30 minutes then serve with tortilla chips.

1 small can chopped ripe
    black olives
1 small can green chilies,
    chopped
2 medium ripe red
    tomatoes, diced
6 green onions with tops,
    diced
½ cup oil and vinegar
    dressing
salt to taste
tortilla chips

Mixing bowl

Tuna or Chicken Dip

Recipe from Dotti Casoria
A favorite of John and Dotti Casoria
Bethany Christian Center, Loganville, Georgia
Jan Crouch's Sister and Brother-in-law

Toss together first 5 ingredients. Scoop out center of cabbage to form a bowl. Serve with crackers.

two 8-ounce cans solid tuna
    or chicken
½ cup broken pecans or
    toasted almond slivers
1 cup green grapes or
    fresh pineapple
    chunks
2 small tender stalks of
    celery, chopped
mayonnaise to taste
1 large leafy cabbage

Large dish
Mixing bowl

Accompaniments

Holiday Eggnog

Recipe from Mrs. C.M. (Dorothy) Ward
A favorite of Dr. C. M. Ward
Stockton, California

Beat sugar and spices into beaten eggs. Stir in chilled orange and lemon juice. Pour into punch bowl, and add ice cream chunks. Pour in ginger ale over all. Sprinkle with nutmeg.

¼ **cup sugar**
½ **teaspoon cinnamon**
¼ **teaspoon ginger**
¼ **teaspoon cloves**
6 well beaten eggs
2 quarts orange juice,
     (may be frozen)
½ **cup lemon juice**
1 quart vanilla ice
     cream (cut in pieces)
1 quart ginger ale

Punch bowl

Christian Radio Pioneer, Dr. C. M. Ward served as speaker
on the Revivaltime radio program for over 25 years.

Accompaniments

Jan's Easy Corn Bread Dressing

Recipe from Jan Crouch
A favorite of Paul and Jan Crouch
Founders and President of TBN
Hosts of Praise the Lord *seen on TBN*

Two days before: Make solid pan of muffin mix (follow instructions on JIFFY™ corn muffin box).
Day before: Melt 2 sticks of butter. Soften almonds in butter, then remove almonds. Soften onion in butter. In large cooking pan, put small layer of Mrs. Cubbison's™ dressing. Crumble small amount of corn bread. Pour some of the onions and almonds over dressing. Pour a little of turkey drippings. Repeat this until all ingredients are layered in large pan. Whip eggs in extra bowl. Pour eggs over whole thing. Mix lightly. Pour more turkey drippings until dressing mixture is soft. Bake until browned on top.

1 package Mrs. Cubbison's™ seasoned dressing (not corn bread dressing)
2 packages JIFFY™ corn muffin mix (not corn bread mix)
2 sticks butter
2 packages slivered almonds (not whole)
1 package frozen chopped onions
4 eggs
drippings from cooked turkey

Large cooking pan
Small bowl

Accompaniments

Betty Jean's Homemade Corn Bread Dressing

Recipe from Betty Jean Robinson
Gospel Songwriter and Recording Artist
Host of Up On Melody Mountain seen on TBN

Mix your cornmeal, buttermilk and your egg for the corn bread. Bake until done. After baking let cool, then crumble well and add celery, onions, and sage to your taste. Then add chicken stock (more if you like your dressing real moist). Pour back into greased skillet or pan and bake for 30 minutes. Delicious!

self-rising cornmeal
buttermilk
1 egg
1 cup celery, chopped
1 cup onions, chopped
sage to your taste
chicken stock

Oven temperature 350°

Large iron skillet or pan

Betty Jean's latest album is Touch Of Heaven.

Accompaniments

Orange Rice Stuffing

Recipe from Dotti Casoria
A favorite of John and Dotti Casoria
Bethany Christian Center, Loganville, Georgia
Jan Crouch's Sister and Brother-in-law

Heat in saucepan butter and onion. Cook until onion is tender but not brown. Add 4 cups water, orange juice, orange rind, celery, salt and poultry seasoning. Bring to boil and stir in instant rice. Cover and remove from heat. Let stand for 5 minutes. Add ½ cup chopped parsley. Fluff with fork.

5⅓ cups instant rice
1 cup butter or margarine
1 onion, chopped
4 cups water
1 cup orange juice
3 tablespoons grated
 orange rind
4 cups celery, chopped
2 tablespoons salt
1 teaspoon poultry
 seasoning
½ cup chopped parsley

Large saucepan

32

Spinach Dip

Recipe from Jan Crouch
A favorite of Paul and Jan Crouch
Founders and President of TBN
Hosts of Praise the Lord seen on TBN

Thaw 1 package frozen chopped spinach and squeeze dry. Combine 1 package Knorr™ Vegetable Soup and Recipe mix., sour cream and mayonnaise until blended. Stir in spinach, water chestnuts, chopped, and green onions. Cover, and chill for 2 hours. Serve with crackers or hollow out a large, round loaf of sourdough bread and reserve the hollowed out bread, cut into squares for dipping.

one 10-ounce package frozen chopped spinach
1 package Knorr™ Vegetable Soup and Recipe mix
1½ cups sour cream
1 cup mayonnaise
one 8-ounce can water chestnuts, chopped
3 cups green onions

Even people that don't care for spinach will think this is delicious.
It is an excellent dip, not in the least typical.

Mama's Nicaraguan Turkey Dressing

Recipe from Mario Murillo
Host of <u>Becoming</u> <u>Armed</u> <u>and</u> <u>Dangerous</u> seen on TBN

Chop potatoes, onion, bell pepper, garlic and pork chops, then brown for about 7 minutes. Add chicken broth, capers, green olives, salt and pepper, then simmer. Best if prepared and refrigerated a few days before serving.

3 diced medium-sized potatoes
1 medium white onion
1 bell pepper
bay leaves
garlic
2 pork chops
1 large can of Swanson™ chicken broth
½ small jar capers
green olives
salt
pepper

Large Saucepan

Julie's Fried Rice

Recipe from Julie Arguinzoni
A favorite of Sonny Arguinzoni
Victory Outreach
La Puente, California

Steam rice then set aside. Fry bacon until crispy then drain and set aside. Dice celery and green onions (use all the green onion) and fry in bacon drippings on medium flame for one minute. Add steamed rice, stir fry, add soy sauce, mix thoroughly. Crumble bacon and add to rice, mix thoroughly. Drain pineapple chunks and fold into rice. Keep on low flame for three minutes then serve.

10 strips of smoked bacon
1 pound of long grain white rice
3 stalks of celery
1 bunch of green onions
¼ cup soy sauce (to taste)
1 small can of pineapple chunks (in juice not syrup)

Frying pan

Cucumber Tortillas

Recipe from Marilyn Hickey
Host of <u>Today</u> <u>with</u> <u>Marilyn</u> seen on TBN

Peel a cucumber and cut into thin spears 5 or 6 inches in length. Heat one tortilla on a hot dry skillet, turning from one side to the other until it is hot and soft. Spread the hot tortillas with mayonnaise. Arrange a line of cucumber spears down the center of your tortillas. Top with lettuce and seasoning. Roll tightly.

cucumber spears
corn tortillas
mayonnaise
shredded lettuce
Spike™
Vegesal™ **or Parsley Patch**™
    Mexican seasoning

Skillet

Salads

Salads

Pineapple Nut Salad

Recipe from Edith Tripp
A favorite of LaVerne, Rob and Terry Tripp
Gospel Songwriters and Recording Artists
Hosts of the LaVerne Tripp Family program seen on TBN

B ring the water to a boil, add gelatin and softened cream cheese. Mix well. Add other ingredients. Pour into pan. Chill and serve.

2 packages lemon gelatin
1 ⅓ cups water
two 3-ounce packages cream cheese, softened
1 can crushed pineapple
1 large can evaporated milk
1 cup chopped nuts
1 jar of cherries

The Tripp's latest album is I'm Still Dancin'.

Hawaiian Strawberry Jell-O™ Salad

Recipe from Rose Shakarian
A favorite of Demos and Rose Shakarian
Full Gospel Businessmen's Fellowship International
Costa Mesa, California

Dissolve strawberry Jell-O™ in hot water. Add frozen sliced strawberries (frozen strawberries will cause Jell-O™ to set slightly). Add bananas, crushed pineapple and walnuts. Separate mixture in half and pour into a square pan or casserole dish. Add a layer of sour cream, Then remaining Jell-O™ mixture and top with rest of the sour cream. Sprinkle with coconut on top.

1 large box of strawberry Jell-O™
1 cup hot water
1 package frozen sliced strawberries
2 mashed bananas
1 small can crushed pineapple
1 pint sour cream
chopped walnuts
shredded coconut

Large mixing bowl
Casserole dish

Cranberry Salad

Recipe from Dodie Osteen
A favorite of the John Osteen family
Lakewood Church, Houston, Texas

Mix all ingredients. Add Cool Whip™ and stir well. Pour in glass serving dish and freeze. Salad can be made 2 to 3 weeks in advance and frozen. When served, let thaw then cut into square pieces. Pretty to serve.

¼ cup lemon juice
1 can Eagle™ brand milk
one 16-ounce can whole cranberries
one 20-ounce can crushed pineapple
1½ cups chopped pecans
8-ounce container of Cool Whip™

13" x 9" Glass dish

Fruit Salad

Recipe from John J. Hinkle
Christ Church, Los Angeles, California

In a large mixing bowl put crushed pineapple and sliced peaches. In medium mixing bowl, mix Jell-O™ with hot water and stir until Jell-O™ is thoroughly dissolved. Cool Jell-O™ with ice cubes and add water to make 3½ cups and pour into large mixing bowl. Peel and chop apple into small pieces and add to large bowl. Cut bananas in half and slice into bowl. Add 3 cups of broken pieces of pecans and the marshmallows, stir only until thoroughly mixed. Pour into container and place in refrigerator for at least 12 hours. This gives the fruit flavors a chance to blend.

one 8½-ounce can crushed
 pineapple (diced small)
one 16-ounce can sliced
 peaches (diced small)
6 large bananas
1 large Delicious apple
one 3-ounce box of
 strawberry Jell-O™
3 cups broken pecan pieces
5 ounces miniature
 marshmallows

Large mixing bowl
Medium mixing bowl

Saucepan

Blueberry Salad

Recipe from Mrs. J. Don (Gwen) George
A favorite of the J. Don George family
Calvary Temple, Irving, Texas

Dissolve lemon Jell-O™ with pineapple juice heated in microwave. Mix blueberries, bananas and pineapple with Jell-O™ mixture. Keep in refrigerator for several hours. Next fold Cool Whip™ with mixture until a pretty light purple color.

1 package lemon Jell-O™
1 cup pineapple juice
1 can blueberries (packed in syrup)
1 cup mashed bananas
one 8-ounce Cool Whip™

Large mixing bowl

Really pretty for your Christmas table.

43

Salads

Mediterranean Salad

Recipe from Dale Evans Rogers
Host of A Date With Dale seen on TBN
A favorite of guests of the Roy Rogers family

In wooden bowl, crush large clove of garlic. Cream one teaspoon salt into the garlic, mixing thoroughly. Add juice of the lemon and cover with oregano leaves. Let stand for 30 minutes. Chop green onions into ½" pieces and add to lemon juice mixture. Tear romaine over all. Sprinkle olive oil generously over the top and toss.

1 bunch romaine lettuce
1 bunch green onions
1 large clove garlic, pressed
1 teaspoon salt
½ teaspoon coarse ground
**   pepper**
juice of 1 lemon
oregano leaves
olive oil to cover top of torn
**   romaine leaves**

Wooden bowl

Dale's latest album is Happy Trails.

Caesar Salad

Recipe from Linda Cherry
A favorite of the Dr. Reginald B. Cherry family
Hosts of Doctor and the Word seen on TBN

For crispy lettuce tear lettuce from head, rinse in cold water, blot dry, wrap in clean dry dish towel and place in refrigerator for approximately 30 minutes. Mix all dressing ingredients and set aside. Tear lettuce into bite size pieces in large salad bowl. Pour dressing over lettuce just before serving. Toss and serve on chilled salad plates.

1 teaspoon garlic powder or
½ teaspoon fresh pressed
garlic
1 squirt anchovy paste
¼ teaspoon pepper mill grind
pepper
1 teaspoon lemon juice, fresh
or concentrate
¼ cup olive oil
⅓ cup grated Parmesan
cheese (low-fat, if
possible)
3 or 4 shakes red wine vinegar
8 to 10 romaine lettuce leaves

Large salad bowl
Salad plates chilled

Salads

Mediterranean Pasta Salad

Recipe from Peter and Patti Lalonde
Peter and his brother, Paul co-host
This Week in Bible Prophecy seen on TBN

Crush the clove of garlic in a large bowl. Whisk in red wine vinegar, oil and juice from the marinated artichoke hearts. Put cooked rotini in the bowl with oil and vinegar mixture. Sprinkle with salt and pepper, Italian seasoning, and Parmesan cheese. Add the olives, diced red pepper, and the artichoke hearts. Toss well. Refrigerate and marinate for 4 hours. Toss again before serving. Salad goes good with barbecued steaks and garlic toast.

rotini pasta
1 can sliced and pitted black
 olives
1 red bell pepper
1 clove garlic
1 small jar marinated
 artichoke hearts
Parmesan cheese
salt and pepper
Italian seasonings (basil,
 oregano)
red wine vinegar
canola or extra virgin oil

Large bowl

Broccoli Salad

Recipe from Mrs. Dave (Brenda) Roever
A favorite of Dave Roever
Host of the <u>Dave Roever</u> program seen on TBN

Cut broccoli flowerets off into mixing bowl and add mayonnaise, sugar, salt, and vinegar. Mix well. Add raisins and sunflower seeds. Best to make in the morning for the evening meal. Stir a couple of times during the day.

2 or more bunches of broccoli
1 cup raisins
1 cup sunflower seeds or
 pecans
¾ cup mayonnaise
¼ cup sugar
½ teaspoon salt
1½ tablespoon brown vinegar

Large mixing bowl

Salads

Chef Salad

Recipe from Dr. Donald Whitaker
A favorite of Don and Helen Whitaker
Host of Calling Dr. Whitaker *seen on TBN*

Wash lettuce, let drain and tear into bite size pieces. Combine all the ingredients. Reserve the asparagus spears for a garnish. Toss with honey lemon dressing. Divide into two portions heaping each onto a large chilled plate. Keep plates in freezer while preparing salad. Lay asparagus spears over the top as garnish.

1 small head leafy green lettuce
1 cup canned garbanzo beans, rinsed
½ cup canned kidney beans, rinsed
½ cup frozen peas, rinse to thaw
2 tablespoons chopped green onion
1 tablespoon hulled sunflower seeds
1 cup unsweetened julienne beets
1 large tomato, in chunks
6 asparagus spears
honey lemon dressing

Large bowl

Barbecue Egg Plant Salad

Recipe from Leon Isaac Kennedy
Actor and Producer
Los Angeles, California

Barbecue egg plant, peppers, and tomatoes over a grill for 10 minutes. Peel vegetables, open and remove seeds from egg plant. Chop vegetables, add onion and parsley. Squeeze lime over everything and enjoy!

Japanese egg plant
green peppers
ripe tomatoes
1 cup chopped onion
1 cup chopped parsley
lime

Barbecue grill

Chicken Salad

Recipe from Mrs. Pat (Dede) Robertson
A favorite of Dr. Pat Robertson
Host of the 700 Club seen on TBN

Mix together and serve on bed of lettuce or in lettuce cup. Mandarin oranges can be substituted for the pineapple, and green grapes can be added to either.

4 cups diced chicken breast (cooked)
one 20-ounce can of diced pineapple
2 cups finely diced celery
1 cup pecan pieces
1 cup mayonnaise (Hellman's™ or Weight Watchers™)

Large mixing bowl

Chinese Salad

Recipe from Tawny Crouch
A favorite of the Paul Crouch, Jr. family
Paul and Jan Crouch's Son and Daughter-in-law and
Grandchildren – Brandon, Brittany and Carra

Marinate chicken overnight in oil, sugar, rice vinegar, onions, salt and Accent™. When ready to eat, mix leaf ingredients and top with chicken sauce and wontons.

5 whole chicken breasts, cooked, deboned, cut into strips
1 head of lettuce
1 bunch spinach
½ cup sesame seeds
½ cup slivered almonds, toasted under broiler
½ package wonton skins, fried crumbled up
⅔ cup oil
½ cup sugar
½ cup rice vinegar
½ cup sliced green onion
1 teaspoon salt
2 teaspoons Accent™

Large salad bowl

Hot Chicken Salad

Recipe from Marilyn McCoo
Vocalist and Recording Artist
Los Angeles, California

Preheat oven. In large bowl combine all ingredients, except chips and cheese. Mix well. Turn into 1 quart baking dish. top with chips and bake for 30 minutes. Top with cheese and bake for 3 minutes longer or until cheese melts.

3 cups cubed chicken
1 cup chopped celery
¾ cup mayonnaise or salad
  dressing
¾ cup slivered almonds,
  toasted
1 tablespoon lemon juice
1 tablespoon chopped onion
2 tablespoons chicken
  flavored instant bouillon
½ cup crushed potato chips
½ cup shredded cheddar
  cheese

Oven temperature 350°

Large bowl
Baking dish

Marilyn's latest Gospel album is The Me Nobody Knows.

Cranberry Salad

Recipe from Natalie Sekulow
(Jay's mother, not pictured)
A holiday favorite of Jay and Pam Sekulow
Christian Advocates Serving Evangelism, Atlanta, Georgia
Host of A Call to Action seen on TBN

Put cranberries in mixing bowl. Add pineapple, sugar and marshmallows. Mix well, then cover. Refrigerate 8 to 10 hours. Before serving, whip the cream and fold into cranberry mix. Add pecans.

1 pound fresh cranberries, chopped fine
½ cup sugar
one 10-ounce can crushed, drained pineapple
1 pound small marshmallows
½ pint whipping cream
1 cup pecans

Salads

Shrimp Salad

Recipe from Mrs. John (Diana) Hagee
A favorite of John Hagee
Cornerstone Church, San Antonio, Texas
Host of Cornerstone and John Hagee Today seen on TBN

Combine cooked pasta and garlic and set aside. Add shrimp, celery, and peas. Then add mayonnaise and fold in pimentos. Salt to taste. Allow to cool in refrigerator up to 3 hours before serving on a bed of lettuce.

2 pounds medium to large shrimp cut in large chunks, cooked
2 teaspoons garlic (fresh and minced)
2 cups celery diced
1 large jar diced pimentos
2 cups small sweet green peas
1 pound thin spaghetti, cooked as directed
1 quart mayonnaise

Medium size bowl

Vegetables

Vegetables

Scalloped Asparagus with Almonds

Recipe from Dr. D. James "Jim" and Anne Kennedy
Coral Ridge Presbyterian Church, Fort Lauderdale, Florida
Host of <u>Coral Ridge Hour</u> seen on TBN

In casserole dish arrange layer of asparagus, cream sauce, cheese, almonds, and crumbs. Repeat until dish is ⅔ full. Bake in hot oven until bubbly and brown on top.

1 can green asparagus, well drained
3 cups cream sauce, well seasoned
1 cup New York state sharp cheese, grated
1 cup almonds, blanched
3 tablespoons grated light bread crumbs

Oven temperature 350°

Medium casserole dish

"I don't have any special recipes for Jim's favorite meal, because he is mostly a 'meat and potatoes' man and everyone knows how to fix those! His favorite meal is rare roast beef, mashed potatoes, and tiny green peas. I wish it were something more exotic!" –Anne

Vegetables

Delicious Sweet Potatoes

Recipe from Mary Brown
A favorite of Dean and Mary Brown
Gospel Songwriters and Recording Artists
Hosts of Music That Ministers seen on TBN

Cook and mash potatoes. Cool, then add granulated sugar, ½ stick margarine, eggs, vanilla and milk. Put into casserole dish. For topping, mix flour, brown sugar, and nuts, then add margarine. Spread on top of potatoes. Bake uncovered for 1 hour (I always check after 45 minutes).

6 medium sweet potatoes or canned yams
1 cup granulated sugar
½ stick margarine
2 eggs beaten
1 teaspoon vanilla
½ can evaporated milk

Topping:
1 cup brown sugar
¼ cup flour
½ stick margarine
1 cup pecans, chopped

Oven temperature 325°

Casserole dish

Dean and Mary's latest album is I Am Determined.

Mater-Taters

Recipe from Ricky Van Shelton
Country and Gospel Recording Artist
Nashville, Tennessee

Melt butter and add oil to skillet. Sauté onions and add parsley. Add tomatoes and potatoes, salt and pepper. Cover and simmer for 30 minutes over medium heat or until potatoes are done.

½ **onion, diced**
¼ **stick butter or margarine**
2 **tablespoons olive oil**
2 **tablespoons parsley**
8 **ounces whole tomatoes,**
     chopped
2 **to 3 medium potatoes, sliced**
salt and pepper to taste

Skillet

Ricky's latest album is <u>Greatest</u> <u>Hits</u> <u>Plus</u>.

Betty Jean's Fried Sweet Potatoes

Recipe from Betty Jean Robinson
Gospel Songwriter and Recording Artist
Host of Up On Melody Mountain seen on TBN

Take your oil and butter and heat slightly, add your sweet potatoes and your sugar and let fry until sugar begins to melt. Do not stir yet and do not let burn. Then add 2 tablespoons of water and stir slightly. Cover and fry until tender. 1 drop vanilla flavoring, optional.

3 large sweet potatoes
¼ cup oil
½ stick butter
1 cup sugar
2 tablespoons water
vanilla (optional)

Large skillet

Betty Jean's latest album is Touch Of Heaven.

Pepper Corn

Recipe from Pat Brock
A favorite of Steve Brock
Gospel Recording Artist
Host of the <u>Steve Brock</u> program seen on TBN

Cook milk, margarine, and cream cheese over medium heat. Then add shoe peg corn and bake for 30 minutes.

¼ cup canned milk
½ stick margarine
6 ounce cream cheese
2 boxes of shoe peg corn or
1 bag shoe peg corn

Oven temperature 350°

8" x 8" casserole dish

Steve's latest album is <u>Going Up With A Shout</u>.

Vegetables

Yellow Squash

Recipe from Gloria Copeland
A favorite of Kenneth and Gloria Copeland
Hosts of <u>Believer's Voice of Victory</u> and
<u>Kenneth Copeland Daily Study</u> seen on TBN

Wash squash, slice thin, ½ inch thick. Use Teflon™ or heavy skillet. Sauté onion in canola and butter mixture. Add squash, cover and cook on low heat until tender. There will be enough water on squash to cook on low heat. Salt sparingly.

3 to 4 yellow squash
1 medium onion
2 tablespoons canola oil
2 tablespoons butter

Teflon™ or heavy skillet

Vegetables

Collards and Corn Bread

Recipe from Evelyn Roberts
A favorite of Dr. Oral and Evelyn Roberts
Oral Roberts University, Tulsa, Oklahoma

Use 2 bunches of collards or other greens. Wash thoroughly 2 or 3 times to remove sand, take out tough stems and discard. Put 2 ham hocks or 1 cup ham chunks in bottom of pot. Add greens and fill ½ full of water. Let greens come to boil then turn fire down and simmer 2½ to 3 hours or until seasoned and tender. Add salt according to taste, when serving. Lift greens out of water into a flat bowl and cut into bite size pieces with a sharp knife. We like to sprinkle pepper sauce or vinegar on our plates.

Corn Bread:
Beat egg in mixing bowl. Add buttermilk, salt, sugar, ⅛ teaspoon baking soda, baking powder, vegetable oil and yellow cornmeal. As you mix add more cornmeal until it reaches a spreading consistency. Set iron skillet on burner. Brush oil on bottom and sides with pastry brush. Pour in corn bread mixture and put in oven. Bake for 20 to 30 minutes or until brown on top and bottom. Take out and turn upside down on plate. Cut in pie wedges. Enjoy hot with Collard greens, sliced tomatoes, green onions, chow chow or pickled relish.

2 bunches collard greens or
turnip and mustard
greens
salt
water
2 ham hocks or
1 cup ham chunks

Corn Bread:
1 egg
1 cup buttermilk
¼ teaspoon salt
½ teaspoon baking soda
2 heaping teaspoons double-
acting baking powder
baking powder
¼ cup vegetable oil

¾ cup yellow cornmeal

Oven temperature

Vegetables

Candied Yams

Recipe from Cindy Way
A favorite of Del Way
Gospel Recording Artist and Pastor of
Calvary Temple, Kerrville, Texas

B eat together eggs, milk, and sugar. Mix together brown sugar, flour, and pecans. Line potatoes in dish. Pour egg mixture over potatoes. Then add brown sugar mixture. Dot pads of butter on top. Bake for 25 minutes. Then add marshmallows on top and bake for 5 minutes more.

2 large cans of yams, drained
1 stick butter
1 package marshmallows
2 eggs
½ cup evaporated milk
¾ cup sugar
1 cup brown sugar
⅓ cup flour
1 cup pecans, chopped

Oven temperature 350°

Casserole dish
Mixing bowl

Del's latest album in <u>You'll</u> <u>Never</u> <u>Be</u> <u>The</u> <u>Same</u>.

Steamed Cabbage

Recipe from Gloria Copeland
A favorite of Kenneth and Gloria Copeland
Hosts of Believer's Voice of Victory and
Kenneth Copeland Daily Study seen on TBN

Cut cabbage in half and core. Lay flat sides on cutting board. Cut into thin slices. Drop into cold water until ready to cook. Melt 2 tablespoons of butter in heavy pot (like soup pot). Add 2 tablespoons canola oil. Use large fork to lift cabbage out of water into butter mixture. Let water drip from cabbage. Cover. Cook on low heat several minutes. There will be enough water left on cabbage to make steam. Use fork to turn cabbage over. Cook until tender. Salt sparingly.

cabbage head
2 tablespoons butter
2 tablespoons canola
salt

Heavy soup pot
Large fork

Aunt Laura's Broccoli Bake

Recipe from Mrs. Jim (Connie) McClellan
A favorite of Jim McClellan
Host of JOY seen on TBN and
Manager of Ch. 24, Portland, Oregon
National Minority TV (A TBN Affiliate)

Place frozen broccoli spears in buttered casserole dish. Mix chicken soup and mayonnaise together and pour over broccoli. Spread grated cheese over the top. Mix bread crumbs with melted butter and sprinkle over the top of all. Bake for 30 minutes uncovered.

4 boxes frozen broccoli spears
1 can cream of chicken soup
1 cup mayonnaise,
  (not Miracle Whip™)
1 package (½ pound or so)
  Monterey Jack cheese,
  grated
1 cup bread crumbs
½ cube butter, melted

Oven temperature 350°

13" x 9" Casserole dish

Soups

Soups

Spilt Pea Soup

Recipe from Dr. Julian Whitaker
A favorite of the Whitaker family
Whitaker Wellness Institute, Newport Beach, California

Soak the peas overnight. Cook all ingredients together in a pot, watching to make sure it does not boil over, until the peas are tender and the rice is done (at least 1 hour).

1½ cups uncooked split peas
8 cups water
1 cup apple juice
1 cup chopped carrots (approximately 3)
½ cup salsa
1 cup chopped yellow onion
1 cup uncooked rice
3 tablespoons vegetable broth seasoning
1 tablespoon tomato paste

Large cooking pot
Bowl for peas

Chili Tex

Recipe from Dale Evans Rogers
Host of A Date With Dale seen on TBN
A favorite of the Roy Rogers family

In baking dish, arrange in alternate layers, chili and beans, onions, and hominy. Top with grated cheese and bake until onions are tender and the cheese is thoroughly melted.

1 can chili and beans
1 can white or yellow hominy
chopped onions
grated cheese

Oven temperature 350°

Baking Dish

Dale's latest album is Happy Trails.

Jessye's Healthy Soup

Recipe from Kathy Hayes
A favorite of Mike and Kathy Hayes
Covenant Church, Carrollton, Texas

Blend all vegetables and ingredients using broth or milk as liquid. May need to use 1 cup of broth at a time before all vegetables can be blended. Pour all ingredients into saucepan and heat until slightly thickened and ready to eat.

4 cups milk or broth
2 large potatoes washed and unpeeled
2 medium carrots
½ fresh spinach
1 small onion
3 garlic cloves
½ cup green beans
1 zucchini
2 mushrooms
4 tablespoons whole wheat flour
4 tablespoons extra virgin olive oil
seasoning to taste using sea salt, soy sauce, pepper
optional Mrs. Dash™ for extra spice

Blender
Large saucepan

Quick, Easy Chili

Recipe from Ruthie Crouch Brown
A favorite of Al Brown, Chief of Staff, TBN
Paul Crouch's Sister and Brother-in-law

Brown meat, onion, green pepper, and mushrooms in skillet. Add other ingredients and simmer for 20 minutes. This is delicious served over rice or any shape of pasta or just plain by itself.

½ **pound extra lean ground beef**
1 **can ranch style beans**
1 **can Mexican style stewed tomatoes**
one 8-ounce can tomato sauce
1 **can water**
1 **medium onion, chopped**
½ **green pepper, chopped**
a few sliced fresh mushrooms (optional)

Large skillet with lid

Beef Stew

Recipe from Robbie Britt's Mom
A favorite of Robbie Britt
Gospel Recording Artist
Riverside, California

Boil meat, diced onions, diced celery, diced carrots, bay leaves, parsley on top of stove until meat is well done and tender. Cool in refrigerator overnight. Next day take pot with cold ingredients and spoon grease off that has come to the top, and throw away. Put pot with ingredients back on stove. Add baby limas (cook until tender). Then add chunked potatoes (cook until done), then add can of green beans and corn. Cook macaroni noodles separate until done. Then add noodles to stew. Warm all stew together and serve hot.

2 packages of stew meat
     (1½ to 2 pounds)
2 packages frozen baby limas
2 cans tomato sauce
1 can diced tomatoes
1 onion
4 celery sticks
2 large carrots
2 cans green beans
2 packages frozen corn
3 cups macaroni noodles
5 medium to large potatoes
3 bay leaves
teaspoon parsley
salt and pepper to taste

Large pot

Robbie's latest album is <u>Robbie</u>.

Soups

Oyster and Artichoke Soup

Recipe from Mrs. Jesse (Cathy) Duplantis
A favorite of Jesse and Cathy Duplantis
Host of the Jesse Duplantis program seen on TBN

In large pot, sauté onions in butter. Add flour and mix until paste. Add chicken broth and milk and mix together. Add all other ingredients and cook on medium heat until oysters curl (do not boil). Turn off heat and allow to set awhile with lid on. Serve hot and enjoy.

2 sticks butter
2 large onions chopped
¾ cup flour
chicken broth 4 cups
    (use bouillon cubes
    and water)
2 cups milk
2 cans artichoke hearts in
    water (mash with hands)
oysters 2 quarts with water,
    or substitute with fresh
    mushrooms that have
    been sautéed in butter
spices: (be generous)
    garlic
    basil
    celery salt
    lemon pepper
    red pepper
    thyme
    season all
    fresh parsley, chopped
    fresh green onions,
        chopped

Large pot

You may substitute main ingredients for almost anything:
broccoli and cheese, crab and cheese, potato and cheese.

Mother's Chili

Recipe from Debra Paget
Houston, Texas
A favorite of many friends in Hollywood, California

In a skillet, sauté onions in butter until yellow and soft. Add beef and brown. Add 1 teaspoon Lawry's™ seasoning salt, pepper, and garlic powder. In pan, put tomatoes (already blended in blender) beef, kidney beans, chili powder, cumin, remaining Lawry's™ salt, garlic powder, pepper, and 1 pinch of sugar. Simmer ½ hour or more. Stir and taste occasionally for additional seasoning. Serve with crackers, raw onions, grated cheddar cheese and canned corn.

1 tablespoon butter or oil
2 cups onion
2 pounds ground beef
1¼ teaspoons Lawry's™
    seasoning salt
1 teaspoon black pepper
2 cans tomatoes (blend)

Optional:
2 cans dark kidney beans
4 to 5 tablespoons chili
    powder
2 teaspoons cumin
1½ teaspoon garlic powder

Skillet
Large saucepan

Debra's numerous movie credits include a starring role in Cecil B. De Mille's production of "The Ten Commandments."

Old Timer's Beef Stew

Recipe from Linda Cherry
A favorite of the Dr. Reginald B. Cherry family
Hosts of Doctor and the Word seen on TBN

Trim all fat from beef tips. Place all ingredients in crock pot or oven roaster. Mix thoroughly. Cover and cook on preferred setting, depending on method of cooking. This is a great recipe for the working wife and/or mother. Doubling this recipe will serve a large group of people. Serve with corn bread or crackers.

2 pounds lean ground beef tips
4 carrots, sliced
3 medium potatoes, cubed
one 28-ounce can stewed tomatoes
½ cup quick-cook tapioca
1 whole clove
2 bay leaves
light salt and pepper

Oven temperature 350° or
Oven roaster or
Crock Pot:
    low heat 11 to 12 hours
    high heat 5 to 6 hours

The secret ingredient that makes this stew like "Old Timer's" is the tapioca.

Ground Turkey Chili

Recipe from Laurie Crouch
A favorite of Matt and Laurie Crouch
Hosts of <u>Real</u> <u>Videos</u> and <u>Kid's</u> <u>Club</u> seen on TBN
Paul and Jan Crouch's Son and Daughter-in-law

Thaw turkey if frozen. Heat butter in large saucepan or casserole dish. Add garlic, sauté for 30 seconds. Then add onion and cook over medium to high heat until onion begins to brown. Add turkey, cook about 5 minutes, stirring until turkey is no longer pink. Add salt, basil, chili powder, thyme, oregano, and black pepper, stirring well. Add tomatoes and beans, undrained. Simmer 10 to 15 minutes, serve hot.

1 pound ground turkey
1 tablespoon butter or margarine
1 clove garlic (minced or pressed)
1 large onion, chopped
1 teaspoon salt
1 teaspoon dried basil leaves
1 teaspoon chili powder
½ teaspoon dried thyme
½ teaspoon oregano leaves
¼ teaspoon black pepper
one 16-ounce can stewed tomatoes
one 16-ounce can Italian kidney beans
Parmesan cheese to sprinkle over individual servings

Large saucepan or casserole dish

Matt, Caylan and I like to put a little sour cream and Parmesan cheese on each serving. This is also great served over a nice hot baked potato or just with some good ol' corn bread.

Soups

Self-Control Chili

Recipe from Mrs. Pat (Dede) Robertson
A favorite of Dr. Pat Robertson
Host of the 700 Club seen on TBN

In large skillet, combine fat, ground soybeans, onion, garlic and brown lightly. Transfer to large pot. Add oregano, cumin seed, chili powder, tomatoes, whole portion of soybeans. Cover with water and bring to boil, lower heat and simmer at least one hour. Ground beef and pork may be substituted for equal amount of the ground soybeans.

2 teaspoons suet, fat or oil
3 cups cooked soybeans, ground
1 large chopped onion
1 clove garlic, minced
1 teaspoon oregano
1 teaspoon cumin seed
6 teaspoons (or more) chili powder
2 medium cans tomatoes
3 cups cooked soybeans or
3 cups cooked chili beans or
1½ cups of both

Large skillet
Large pot

Turkey Chowder

Recipe from Karen Kelley
Gospel Recording Artist
Glendale, California

Fry bacon slices. Remove from fat and cool. Crumble later. Fry potatoes, onions, and celery in drippings. Put all ingredients in the crock pot withholding the half and half until closer to serving time. You can put crock pot on high or low depending on time allowed. Option: for lower fat, leave out bacon drippings and half and half. Boil potatoes, onions and celery in broth and use milk instead of half and half.

8 slices chopped bacon, plus drippings
2 cups chopped onion
4 cups potatoes cubed or mashed
½ cup chopped celery
2 cups broth
1 can creamed corn
1 can whole corn
4 cups left-over turkey chopped
1 pint half and half
salt and white pepper
shredded carrots

Crock pot or
Big kettle

Karen's latest album is <u>*The Desire Of My Heart*</u>.

Broccoli Cheese Soup

Recipe from Reba Rambo McGuire
A favorite of Dony and Reba Rambo McGuire
Gospel Songwriters and Recording Artists
Nashville, Tennessee

Heat butter and sauté onions. Add water and bouillon cubes. Bring to a boil and gradually add noodles and salt. Cook uncovered for 3 minutes. Stir in broccoli and garlic powder. Cook for 3 minutes and add milk, cheese, and pepper. Stir constantly until cheese melts.

1 tablespoon butter or margarine
¾ cup onion, chopped
6 cups water
6 chicken bouillon cubes
8 ounces fine egg noodles
1 teaspoon salt
two 10-ounce packages frozen, chopped broccoli
⅛ teaspoon garlic powder
6 cups milk
1 pound pasteurized American cheese
pepper to taste

Large saucepan

Dony and Reba's latest album is Suddenly.

Seafood Extravaganza

Recipe from Mrs. Frederick K.C. (Betty) Price
A favorite of Dr. Frederick K.C. Price
Crenshaw Christian Center, Los Angeles, California
Host of <u>Ever Increasing Faith</u> seen on TBN

Cook chicken breasts in 5 quarts of boiling water seasoned well with seasoning salt and pepper to taste. Remove from water when done, let cool. Then cut up in small pieces—save broth. While chicken is cooking, shell, remove vein, clean shrimp and cut into 3 pieces; shell and cut up crab meat. Slice polish sausage in small pieces and sauté. Chop onion and green pepper and sauté in cooking oil in a 10 or 12 quart pan. Cut up the okra and add to the onion and green pepper and continue to cook until done. Slice and add canned tomatoes with juice and chicken broth (add extra water to broth to fill the pot ¾ full). Mix flour with ¼ cup of water for thickening and add to broth. Add Worcestershire sauce and bay leaves. Let boil, then simmer for 30 minutes. Add shrimp and cook 2 minutes, then add cooked chicken breasts, crab meat, and sautéed polish sausage and let boil a few minutes. Turn off heat and add gumbo file. Serve over cooked rice.

2 dozen fresh jumbo shrimp
¼ pound fresh Alaskan
 crab meat
6 polish sausage links
6 chicken breasts
1 large onion
1 large green onion
1 large can whole tomatoes
1 package frozen or fresh
 whole okra
2 bay leaves
1 tablespoon Worcestershire
 sauce
2 tablespoons flour
4 tablespoons cooking oil
3 tablespoons gumbo file
salt or seasoning salt and
pepper to taste

10-Quart pot

Soups

Vegetable Soup

Recipe from Cindy Way
A favorite of Del Way
Gospel Recording Artist and Pastor of
Calvary Temple, Kerrville, Texas

Brown ground beef. Boil potatoes until tender. Add all ingredients into large pot. Cook 30 to 45 minutes on low heat. Always great the second day. Serve with corn bread and salad. Del loves this on a cold day.

1 pound ground beef (optional)
4 potatoes (peeled and quartered)
1 large can whole tomatoes
1 can rotel tomatoes (diced)
1 can Campbell's™ beef broth
1 can water
2 can Veg-all™ mixed vegetables

Large pot
Skillet

Del's latest album is You'll Never Be The Same.

Chicken Soup

Recipe from Jan Crouch
A favorite of Paul and Jan Crouch
Founders and President of TBN
Hosts of <u>Praise</u> <u>the</u> <u>Lord</u> seen on TBN

Cover hen in pan with water. Cook the day before. Cook until it falls off the bones. Separate bones from meat. In pan, cook noodles in chicken soup. Cook wild rice in extra pan, then combine together.

1 whole fat hen chicken
salt and pepper
3 chicken necks
(healing in neck)
1 package frozen onions
6 chicken flavor bouillon
cubes
wild rice or noodles

Very large pot
Extra pan for rice

Soups

Conch Chowder

Recipe from Dr. and Mrs. Myles Munroe
Bahamas Faith Ministries International
Nassau, Bahamas
Host of the <u>Myles Munroe</u> program seen on TBN

Conch and ham bone or salt beef pieces placed in 4 cups water. Cover and boil until conch is tender. Remove bone and discard fried out bacon, add onions, green pepper, and celery. Sauté until light brown, stirring to prevent burning. Add tomato paste or catsup, tomatoes to sauce. Stir well for 1 minute. Add this mixture to pot with conch. Add remaining ingredients and simmer until vegetables are at desired tenderness. Season to taste. Serve hot.

8 large or 12 medium conchs, diced or ground
2 celery stalks
1 pound tomatoes
6 large potatoes, diced
¼ to ½ pound bacon or salt beef, cut into cubes
2 large onions, chopped
1 green pepper, diced
2 to 4 bay leaves
2 to 4 tablespoons thyme
2 tablespoons butter or margarine
4 carrots, diced
2 medium tomatoes or 2 teaspoons tomato paste or catsup
1 ham bone with meat bits (optional)
seasoned salt and pepper to taste

Skillet
Large pot

Jacob's Lentil Soup

Recipe from Jan Crouch
A favorite of Paul and Jan Crouch
Founders and President of TBN
Hosts of <u>Praise</u> <u>the</u> <u>Lord</u> seen on TBN

Add lentils to 1½ quarts of boiling salted water. Boil at medium for approximately 1 hour. In separate pan combine olive oil, tomatoes (crushed with potato masher or by hand), onion, garlic, parsley, and celery. Add additional water, stir well and frequently to avoid scorching. When mixture comes to boil, simmer at medium for about 1 hour. At end of this time add vegetable mixture to boiled lentils. Stir well and let stand for several hours before serving. Reheat carefully, stirring well to avoid scorching. Serve with grated Parmesan cheese.

¼ pound washed dry lentils
3 tablespoons olive oil
salt and pepper to taste
2 large cans stewed tomatoes
1 large onion, chopped or
**   1 package frozen onions**
1 clove garlic, minced
¼ tablespoon finely
**   chopped fresh parsley**
1 stalk fresh celery,
**   chopped**
a little sugar, to taste
Parmesan cheese, grated

Large pot
Saucepan

Esau's Stew

Recipe from Mrs. Hugh (Kathy) Ross
A favorite of the Dr. Hugh Ross family
Host of Reasons to Believe seen on TBN

Sauté steak, celery and onions in cooking sherry . Then add 6 cups water and lentils. Cook 20 minutes over medium heat (lower heat if necessary). Add canned tomatoes with juice, barley, and spices. Simmer 45 minutes. Add fresh tomato, carrots, and squash. Simmer 20 minutes more or until vegetables are tender enough to suit you.

cooking sherry
¾ pound round steak, diced and de-fatted
¾ cup celery, chopped
¾ cup onion, chopped
1 cup red lentils
1 can tomatoes, chopped
1 fresh tomato, chopped
¾ cup barley
2 teaspoons seasoning salt
10 twists fresh ground pepper
½ teaspoon garlic powder
1 teaspoon crushed rosemary
2 carrots, chopped
1 small zucchini, chopped
1 small yellow squash, chopped
6 cups water

6-Quart cooking pot

Vegetable Beef Soup

Recipe from Naomi Ridings
A Christmas favorite of the Bernard Ridings family
Northland Cathedral, Kansas City, Missouri
Paul Crouch's Sister and Brother-in-law

Brown meat in hot oil. Add bone, water, and seasonings. Cover and simmer 2 hours or cook in pressure cooker for 30 minutes. Add vegetables, noodles, and remaining ingredients. Simmer for 1 hour longer. Add water if needed.

2 pounds beef stew meat
1 knuckle bone
6 cups water
2 cups tomato or V-8™ juice
1 onion, chopped
1 tablespoon salt
2 tablespoons Worcestershire
    sauce
1½ teaspoons kitchen
    bouquet
¼ teaspoon chili powder
2 bay leaves
1 cup (or more) celery
carrots
potatoes
cabbage
½ green pepper left uncut
1 package Lipton™
    vegetable soup mix
¼ cup barley
1 cup noodles
1 can beef broth
1 tablespoon beef base

Skillet
Large pot with lid

Soups

French Market Soup

Recipe from Mrs. Greg (Cathe) Laurie
A favorite of the Greg Laurie Family
Harvest Christian Fellowship, Riverside, California
Host of A New Beginning seen on TBN

Carefully wash beans and rinse them removing any foreign particles. Soak them in water with 1 teaspoon salt overnight. Drain the beans and place them in a large soup pot with 1 quart of water, the hamhock, and bay leaves. Cover and bring to a boil, then reduce the heat and simmer 1½ to 2 hours or until tender. You may need to add water. Add 1 quart of tomatoes, the diced onion, garlic, celery. Add salt and the cayenne pepper to taste. Simmer uncovered 1 hour. Add the sausage and chicken thighs. Cook 30 to 40 minutes until the chicken is very tender. Remove the skin and bones from the chicken. Return the meat to the pot. Adjust seasoning to taste. Serve with French bread.

2 cups, 15 bean gourmet (or a combination of your choice of dry beans)
1 ham hock
2 bay leaves
1 onion, diced
1 quart cut ripe tomatoes
3 large garlic cloves, peeled and crushed
6 stalks celery, chopped
1 pound smoked sausage (Polish kielbasa is great for this) cut in slices
4 to 5 chicken thighs
salt and cayenne pepper

Large soup pot

Cream of Carrot Soup

Recipe from Leon Isaac Kennedy
Actor/Producer
Los Angeles, California

Steam carrots until soft. Put carrots and juice in a blender and liquefy until smooth. Add half and half and seasonings. Heat 10 minutes and enjoy!

3 pounds carrots
1½ cups half and half
¼ teaspoon cumin
½ teaspoon garlic powder
salt
pepper

Blender
Large soup pan

Soups

Oyster Bisque

Recipe from Ron and Linda Dryden.
Cathedral of Praise, Oklahoma City, Oklahoma
Parents of Tawny Crouch (Mrs. Paul Crouch, Jr.)

Sauté onion in butter, stir in flour, salt, pepper, celery salt, and parsley. Cook until bubbly. Remove from heat. Stir in milk gradually. Bring to a boil, for 1 minute. Stir in oysters and liquid. Heat to serving temperature. Serve sprinkled with minced parsley.

1 teaspoon grated onion
1 tablespoon butter
1 teaspoon salt
⅛ teaspoon pepper
⅛ teaspoon celery salt
2 teaspoons finely minced
  parsley
one 8-ounce can whole oysters
1 tablespoon flour
2 cups milk

Large saucepan

"Ron is a gourmet cook!" –Jan Crouch

90

Casseroles

Casseroles

Sweet Potato Casserole

Recipe from Pat Brock
A favorite of Steve Brock
Gospel Recording Artist
Host of the <u>Steve Brock</u> program seen on TBN

Mix together sweet potatoes, sugar, milk, eggs, vanilla, margarine, and coconut. Then mix in separate bowl light brown sugar, self-rising flour, pecans, and margarine. Mix well and spread on top. Bake for 30 minutes.

3 cups sweet potatoes
1 cup sugar
½ cup milk
2 eggs beaten
1 teaspoon vanilla
½ stick margarine
½ cup coconut

Topping:
1 cup light brown sugar
½ cup self-rising flour
1 cup pecans
1 stick margarine

Oven temperature 350°

12" x 8" Pyrex™ pan

Steve's latest album is <u>Going Up With A Shout</u>.

Casseroles

Mexican Casserole

Recipe from Mary Purkey
A favorite of Mike Purkey
Gospel Recording Artist and Pastor of
Lenexa Christian Center, Lenexa, Kansas

Brown meat and add onion and garlic. Cook until onion is soft. Add sauce and chili beans. Stir well. Add 1 package of enchilada seasoning. Cook until well blended. Simmer for 20 minutes. Line baking dish with uncooked corn tortillas. Add half of the meat mixture on top of shells, then add cheese. Then repeat one more time. Bake for 35 minutes.

2 pounds ground beef
1 cup tomato sauce
1 can enchilada sauce, mild
1 can chili beans
1 pound Monterey Jack
    cheese, grated
1 package corn tortillas
garlic salt or fresh garlic,
    minced
1 onion chopped
1 package enchilada
    seasoning

Oven temperature 350°

13" x 9" Baking pan

Mike's latest albums are <u>Let's Have Church</u> and
<u>The Good News Is The Bad News Is Wrong</u>.

Mixed Vegetable Casserole

Recipe from Mrs. Mike (DeAnne) Barber
A favorite of Mike, Brandon, Brittany and Bethany Barber
Mike is host of <u>Proclaim</u> seen on TBN

Cook vegetables and celery until tender, drain. Place in greased casserole dish. Combine cheese, mayonnaise and onion. Mix thoroughly and spread over vegetables. Combine margarine and crackers. Sprinkle over top and bake for 30 minutes.

1 large package frozen mixed vegetables, 20 ounces
1 cup celery, chopped
1 cup grated cheddar cheese
1 cup mayonnaise
1 medium onion, chopped
½ cup margarine, melted
34 Ritz™ crackers, crushed

Oven temperature 350°

13" x 9" Casserole dish

Casseroles

Squash Casserole

Recipe from Randy Travis
A favorite of Randy and Lib Travis
Country Singer and Recording Artist
Nashville, Tennessee

Cook squash and onion until tender. Drain and mash. Add salt and pepper to taste. Add soup, carrots, onion, and sour cream. Place layer of crumbs in bottom of baking dish. Pour mixture over crumbs. Spread a layer of crumbs over top. Dot with butter. Bake for 30 to 35 minutes.

2 pounds yellow squash
1 can cream of chicken soup
2 carrots, grated
1 small onion, chopped
1 cup sour cream
½ package seasoned bread
**   crumbs**
butter

Oven temperature 350°

Casserole dish

Salmon Casserole

Recipe from Dottie McDowell
A favorite of Josh McDowell
Host of the <u>Josh</u> <u>McDowell</u> program seen on TBN

Mix all ingredients together. Pour into a baking pan and bake at 350° degrees for one hour. Serves 4 to 6 people.

1 can pink salmon
½ cup mayonnaise
1 beaten egg
1 cup dry bread crumbs
½ cup chopped onion
½ cup chopped green pepper
1 can cream of celery soup
1 teaspoon lemon juice
1 teaspoon salt

Oven temperature 350°

Baking pan

Hash Brown Casserole

Recipe from Mary Brown
A favorite of Dean and Mary Brown
Gospel Songwriters and Recording Artists
Hosts of Music That Ministers seen on TBN

Place potatoes in 9" x 12" glass dish. In sauce pan, mix ½ cup butter, chicken soup, grated cheese, sour cream, onion and salt. Heat and pour over potatoes. Mix crushed corn flakes with butter and sprinkle over top of potatoes. Bake for 35 minutes.

32 ounce frozen hash brown potatoes
½ cup melted butter
one 10-ounce can cream of chicken soup
12 ounces grated American cheese or melted Cheese Whiz™
8 ounces sour cream
1 teaspoon salt
½ small chopped onion
2 cups crushed cornflakes
¼ cup melted butter

Oven temperature 350°

12" x 9" Baking dish
Saucepan

Dean and Mary's latest album is I Am Determined.

Chicken, Broccoli and Rice Casserole

Recipe from Dotti Casoria
A favorite of John and Dotti Casoria
Bethany Christian Center, Loganville, Georgia
Jan Crouch's Sister and Brother-in-law

Cook broccoli as directed on package, drain. Mix with all other ingredients,but only use ½ can cheese soup. Top with remaining cheese soup and cook for 15 to 20 minutes, until bubbly.

two 13-ounce cans deboned chicken, may use fresh boiled chicken
2 packages frozen chopped broccoli
2 cups cooked rice
1 can cream of mushroom soup
1 can cream of chicken soup
½ cup chopped onion
½ cup chopped celery
1 can cheddar cheese soup

Oven temperature 350°

Large casserole dish

Casseroles

Asparagus and Peas Casserole

Recipe from Dotti Casoria
A favorite of John and Dotti Casoria
Bethany Christian Center, Loganville, Georgia
Jan Crouch's Sister and Brother-in-law

Drain asparagus and half of the liquid from the peas. Mix in casserole dish with golden mushroom soup. Top with crushed crackers and bake until crackers begin to brown and liquid is bubbly.

1 large can small early peas
1 large can asparagus
1 can golden mushroom soup
cheese crackers

Oven temperature 350°

Casserole dish

Yellow Squash Casserole

Recipe from Nancy Harmon
Gospel Songwriter and Recording Artist
Host of <u>Love Special</u> seen on TBN

Slice and dice squash into fourths. Fry squash in butter about 10 minutes or until tender, not soggy. Salt and pepper to taste. Add Lawry's™ garlic salt. Mix in crumbled Ritz™ crackers. Then add cheese. Cook over medium heat until all cheese is melted and mixed thoroughly. Stir to avoid sticking. Do not over stir.

8 medium squash
4 green onions, chopped
2 tablespoons margarine
1 tablespoon Lawry's™
    garlic salt
Ritz™ crackers, crumbled
1½ cups grated cheddar
    cheese
salt and pepper to taste

Casserole dish

Nancy's latest album is <u>Ready</u>.

Casseroles

Broccoli and Tuna Casserole

Recipe from Mrs. C.M. (Dorothy) Ward
A favorite of Dr. C. M. Ward
Stockton, California

Boil broccoli for 10 minutes, no salt. Drain and arrange on shallow baking dish. Cover with tuna. Mix soup and mayonnaise and pour over tuna. Sprinkle with bread crumbs and top with Parmesan cheese. Bake for 20 minutes. Serve over rice.

½ pound broccoli
one 7-ounce can tuna
1 can condensed cream
**   chicken soup**
⅓ cup mayonnaise
⅓ cup fine bread crumbs
Parmesan cheese

Oven temperature 350°

Shallow casserole baking dish

Christian Radio Pioneer, Dr. C. M. Ward served as speaker on the Revivaltime radio program for over 25 years.

Ranch Style Lentil Casserole

Recipe from Dr. Philip and Hazel Crouch
Managers Ch. 58, Irving, Texas, and Pastor of
Trinity Christian Center Church of Irving, Texas
Paul Crouch's Brother and Sister-in-law

Simmer 1 pound of lentils in 5 cups of water with 1 teaspoon of salt (or more if desired) for 20 to 30 minutes. Brown beef in small amount of oil. Drain off any fat. Combine in baking dish. Stir in remaining ingredients. Bake for 30 minutes.

1 pound ground beef
1 pound lentils
  (makes 4 cups cooked)
1 package onion soup mix
1 cup catsup
1 teaspoon prepared mustard
1 teaspoon vinegar
1 cup water
1 teaspoon salt

Oven temperature 400°

Baking dish

Casseroles

Mexican Casserole (King Ranch)

Recipe from Debra Paget
Houston, Texas
A favorite of many friends in Hollywood, California

Cook chicken in water with the salt, pepper and the bay leaf. Remove cooked chicken, keep ¾ cup of chicken stock. Remove skin of chicken and cut chicken into large bite size pieces, set aside. Combine soups, chicken stock, tomatoes, Salt and pepper to taste. Mix well. In casserole dish make 3 layers as follows. 1st, torn tortillas (cover bottom of pan). 2nd, chicken. 3rd, tomato mixture. 4th, chopped onions. 5th, grated cheese. Repeat 2 times more ending with cheese on top. Bake for 45 minutes, cheese will bubble.

4 chicken breasts
2 teaspoons salt
1 teaspoon pepper
1 bay leaf
1 can condensed cream of
mushroom soup
1 can condensed cream of
chicken soup
1 can (10½ ounces) Rotel
tomatoes with green
chilies
3 cups grated sharp cheese
¾ cup chicken stock
additional salt and pepper
12 to 14 tortillas torn in small
pieces
2 onions chopped

Oven temperature 350°

3-Quart casserole pan or dish

Debra's numerous movie credits include a starring role in Cecil B. De Mille's production of "The Ten Commandments."

Beef and Pork

Beef and Pork

Hamburgers Hawaiian

Recipe from Mrs. Jack (Anna) Hayford
A favorite of Dr. Jack Hayford
Church on the Way, Van Nuys, California
Host of Living Way seen on TBN

Combine evaporated milk with ground beef, chopped onion, cracker crumbs and seasoned salt. Form six 4" individual patties by pressing each one between wax paper. Brown patties in skillet in a little oil. Pour out oil. Cover hamburgers with sauce. Simmer on low heat for 15 minutes.

Sweet and sour sauce:
Drain can of pineapple chunks, saving pineapple juice. Combine pineapple juice and water to make 1 cup. Mix with cornstarch, vinegar, brown sugar and soy sauce in pan. Heat until thickened and clear. Add pineapple chunks and chopped green onion. Pour over burgers and serve.

⅔ cup undiluted evaporated milk
1½ pounds ground beef
½ cup chopped onions
⅔ cup cracker crumbs
1 teaspoon seasoned salt

Sweet and sour sauce:
13½-ounce can pineapple chunks
2 tablespoons cornstarch
3 tablespoons vinegar
¼ cup brown sugar
2 tablespoons soy sauce
1 cup coarsely chopped green peppers

Large skillet
Saucepan

"MORE"

Recipe from Maralee Jones
A favorite of Jay Jones
Host of Music of Praise heard worldwide on
KTBN Super Power Shortwave Radio

Brown hamburger and onion together. Drain excess fat. Add remaining ingredients. Layer noodles and sauce twice. Grate Velveeta™ cheese over top of casserole. Bake for 25 minutes or until cheese is thoroughly melted.

1 pound lean hamburger
1 onion chopped
1 can tomato soup
1 can mushroom soup
1 can whole kernel corn
    (drained)
1 can peas (drained)
one 8-ounce package of wide
    noodles (cooked and
    drained)
Velveeta™ cheese

Oven temperature 350°

9" x 13" Pan

Jan's Meat Loaf

Recipe from Jan Crouch
A favorite of Paul and Jan Crouch
Founders and President of TBN
Hosts of Praise the Lord seen on TBN

Mix eggs. Add ground beef, sour cream, onions, crushed cracker crumbs, cheddar cheese and Lawry's™ sauce. Shape together into a loaf. Cover top with ketchup. Bake for 1 to 1½ hours until done and brown on top.

3 pounds of lean ground beef
3 eggs
1 pint sour cream
2 cups grated medium sharp
    cheddar cheese
2 jars Lawry's™ sweet and
    sour sauce
1 package frozen onions
2 cups Waverly Wafer™
    crackers
ketchup

Oven temperature 350°

Medium baking dish

"Matt used to hide it under the bed so that nobody else could get any."

Brisket

Recipe from Bonnie R. Sheaffer
A favorite of Dr. Daniel T. Sheaffer
Crossroads Cathedral, Oklahoma City, Oklahoma
Hosts of The Answer seen on TBN

In large pan, put bay leaves under brisket. Add 1 cup water, 1 bottle Worcestershire sauce, 1 bottle Wishbone™ dressing and marinate overnight. Bake at 250° for 6 hours.

large beef brisket
3 bay leaves
1 bottle Worcestershire sauce
1 bottle Wishbone™ Italian
**   salad dressing**
1 cup water

Oven temperature 250°

Large pan

Hamburger Stroganoff

Recipe from Reeni Fenholt
A favorite of Jeff Fenholt
Contemporary Gospel Recording Artist
Hosts of <u>Highway</u> <u>to</u> <u>Heaven</u> seen on TBN

In large skillet cook beef and onion in butter until onion in tender. Stir in flour, salt, garlic salt, pepper and mushrooms. Cook 5 minutes, stirring constantly. Remove from heat, stir in soup; simmer uncovered 10 minutes. Stir in sour cream, heat through. Serve over noodles. Sprinkle with snipped parsley.

1 pound ground beef
1 medium onion
  (chopped ½ cup)
¼ cup butter or margarine
2 tablespoons flour
1 teaspoon salt
1 teaspoon garlic salt or 1
  garlic clove
¼ teaspoon pepper
1 can mushrooms (drained)
1 can condensed cream of
  mushroom soup
1 cup dairy sour cream to
  taste
2 cups hot cooked noodles
snipped parsley

Large skillet

Jeff's latest album is <u>Jesus</u> <u>50's</u>.

Beef and Pork

Hobo Dinner

Recipe from Edith Tripp
A favorite of the LaVerne Tripp family
Gospel Songwriters and Recording Artists
Hosts of The LaVerne Tripp Family program seen on TBN

Lay aluminum foil on pan. Place beef, sliced potato, onion, bell pepper, salt and pepper. Bake in oven for 1 hour. Serve with rice.

¼ pound ground beef
1 big potato
1 sliced onion
sliced bell pepper
salt and pepper

Oven temperature 375°

Aluminum foil
Baking pan

"Since LaVerne and I are on the run so much, one of my favorite and quick things to make is Hobo Dinner." –Edith

Beef and Pork

Hamburger Stroganoff

Recipe from Karen Wheaton
Gospel Recording Artist
A favorite of the Wheaton Family
Decatur, Alabama

Cook egg noodles according to directions on package. Brown ground beef, drain fat. Over low heat sauté onions and garlic in oil. Add beef, salt and pepper to taste. Add mushrooms and soup. Let it get good and hot, then add sour cream. Heat thoroughly. Serve over egg noodles.

1 pound ground beef
¾ cup onion (chopped)
¾ teaspoon crushed garlic
2 tablespoons oil
salt and pepper
8-ounce can mushrooms
1 can cream of chicken soup
one 8-ounce sour cream
1 bag medium egg noodles

Saucepan
Skillet

Karen's latest album is <u>Remembering</u>.

Beef and Pork

Lib's Electric Pan Fry Meat Loaf

Recipe from Randy Travis
A favorite of Randy and Lib Travis
Country Singer and Recording Artist
Nashville, Tennessee

Mix ground beef and pork, onions, eggs, 1 can stewed tomatoes, cracker crumbs, and salt and pepper. Shape into loaf. Place in center of greased electric fry pan. Peel and quarter potatoes, place around sides of meat loaf with thick sliced carrots. Place bell pepper rings on top of meat loaf. Pour other can of stewed tomatoes over meat loaf and potatoes. Cook for 1 hour until done.

1¼ pounds ground beef
¼ pound ground pork
1 cup onions finely chopped
2 eggs
two 14-ounce can stewed
   tomatoes
¾ cup fine cracker crumbs
salt and pepper to taste
5 medium potatoes
3 medium carrots
3 bell pepper rings

Pan temperature 350°

Electric frying pan
Large mixing bowl

Rock Salt Prime Rib

Recipe from Ron and Linda Dryden
Cathedral of Praise, Oklahoma City, Oklahoma
Parents of Tawny Crouch (Mrs. Paul Crouch, Jr.)

Cover bottom of pan with rock salt. Sprinkle ½ cup water over rock salt. Put prime rib in pan. Cover prime rib completely with rock salt. Bake uncovered at 500° for 12 minutes for each pound. Remove from oven. Hammer off rock salt and serve. (Note: rock salt may be used over and over.)

rock salt
prime rib
½ cup water

Oven temperature 500°

Large roasting pan

"Ron is a gourmet cook!" –Jan Crouch

Beef and Pork

Roast with Potatoes and Carrots

Recipe from Cindy Way
A favorite of Del Way
Gospel Recording Artist and Pastor of
Calvary Temple, Kerrville, Texas

Trim fat off roast, rub into meat on both sides seasoning salt and pepper. Then flour and brown on both sides in a skillet of vegetable oil. Transfer to roaster and add all ingredients except potatoes and carrots. Cover, cook for 2 hours. Then add vegetables and cook for 45 minutes or until roast and vegetables are tender. Serve with French green beans or corn, tossed salad and rolls.

3 to 4 pound shoulder roast, or chuck roast
1 teaspoon pepper
2 teaspoons Lawry's ™ seasoning salt
2 cans Campbell's™ cream of mushroom soup
3 tablespoons vegetable oil
3 tablespoons flour
1 package Lipton™ onion soup
1 bell pepper, sliced
2 cans water
6 medium potatoes, peeled and quartered
6 carrots, cut in 2" pieces

Oven temperature 350°

Large skillet
Oven pot roaster

Del's latest album is <u>You'll</u> <u>Never</u> <u>Be</u> <u>The</u> <u>Same</u>.

Glorious Gloria Hash

Recipe from Mrs. Jess (Doris Cummins) Moody
A favorite of the Dr. Jess Moody family
Shepherd of the Hills Church, Porter Ranch, California
Host of the Jess Moody program seen on TBN

Lightly brown onions and green pepper in small amount of cooking oil. Add meat and stir lightly browning and mixing. Drain off excess liquid. Add mashed tomatoes and juice with one medium can tomato juice and mushrooms. Simmer covered for 30 minutes. Meanwhile, cook and drain noodles, add cheese and mix lightly until melted. Mix meat and tomato mixture with noodles and cheese mixture. Serve hot with garlic bread.

2 to 3 small onions, chopped
1 large green pepper, chopped
2 pounds ground beef
1 large can tomatoes with juice
1 small can mushrooms, drained
1 large package noodles, cooked, drained
1 small package of Velveeta™ cheese cut into cubes
1 medium can tomato juice

Large skillet or
Electric frying pan

Can be prepared on stove and later heated up in oven as leftovers, by adding small amount of tomato juice.

Frito™ Pie

Recipe from Pat Avanzini
A favorite of Dr. John Avanzini
Host of <u>Biblical</u> <u>Economics</u> seen on TBN

L ayer in the following order:
Fritos™, chili, onion, and cheese.
Repeat this order until all ingredients
are used up. Make cheese the last on
top. Bake until the cheese is bubbly.

1 can chili
1 small onion, diced
1 bag dip size Fritos™
Grated cheddar cheese

Oven temperature 350°

Casserole dish

Round Steak with Rich Gravy

Recipe from Meadowlark Lemon
Host of the Meadowlark Lemon program seen on TBN

Sprinkle one side of meat with half the flour; pound in. Turn meat and pound in remaining flour. Cut meat into 6 to 8 serving pieces. Melt shortening in large skillet. Brown meat in shortening over medium heat, about 15 minutes. Sprinkle onion soup mix over meat. Mix water and soup; pour over meat. Cover tightly; simmer 1½ to 2 hours or until tender. Place meat on warm platter. Heat remaining gravy mixture to boiling, stirring constantly; pour over meat.

3 pound beef round steak,
    (top round, bottom
    round or sirloin tip)
    1" thick
1 envelope dry onion soup
½ cup water
1 can condensed cream of
    mushroom soup
flour

Large skillet with lid

Beef and Pork

Beef Stroganoff

Recipe from Ron and Linda Dryden
Cathedral of Praise, Oklahoma City, Oklahoma
Parents of Tawny Crouch (Mrs. Paul Crouch, Jr.)

Sauté mushrooms, onion, pepper in 4 tablespoons butter. Remove from skillet. Cut meat into 2" strips, ¼ " wide. melt 4 tablespoons butter in skillet. Toss strips of meat in flour, coating thoroughly. Brown meat in butter. Add salt and 2 cups consommé liquid. Simmer, stirring occasionally until meat is tender, about 1½ hours. Add mushrooms, onion, bell pepper and sour cream to meat mixture. Serve over white rice or egg noodles.

**2 pounds round steak
(trim fat and tenderized)
½ pound fresh sliced
mushrooms
1 large onion
1 chopped green bell pepper
½ cup butter
2 cups consommé liquid
1 cup sour cream**

Skillet

"Ron is a gourmet cook!" –Jan Crouch

Montana Baked Ham

Recipe from Mrs. Rick (Cindy) Godwin
A favorite of the Rick Godwin family
Eagle's Nest Christian Fellowship, San Antonio, Texas
Host of <u>Reaching Higher</u> seen on TBN

Stud the ham with cloves. Mix in blender the sugar, pineapple juice, crushed pineapple and mustard. Place ham on rack in roasting pan. Pour sauce over ham. Bake for 1 hour at 350°, reduce heat to 300° and cook for 2 hours. Baste ham often with mixture. As juice boils down, add ginger ale. You may remove rack and place ham in juice for the last hour of cooking if you wish.

ham
whole cloves
1½ cups brown sugar
1 teaspoon mustard
2 cups pineapple juice
2 cups crushed pineapple
ginger ale

Oven temperature 350°

Roasting pan

Beef and Pork

Taco Meat

Recipe from Ruthie Crouch Brown
A favorite of Al Brown, Chief of Staff, TBN
and of all the kids and grandkids
Paul Crouch's Sister and Brother-in-law

Brown ground beef in skillet. Drain off any fat. Add tomato paste, sauce, spices and water. Mix all together and let simmer for 20 minutes. This makes a wonderful filling not only for tacos but also on hamburger buns or as the meat for other casseroles. It's better when reheated.

3 pounds extra, extra lean ground beef
2½ teaspoons salt
3 teaspoons sugar
3 teaspoons chili powder
1 teaspoon onion powder
½ teaspoon or more garlic powder
one 6-ounce can tomato paste
one 8-ounce can tomato sauce
1 can water

Large skillet

Beef and Pork

Rice and Pigeon Peas with Pork
(Arroz con Gandules y carne de Cerdo)

Recipe from Julie Arguinzoni
A favorite of Sonny Arguinzoni
Victory Outreach
La Puente, California

In a large sauce pan add oil or lard and brown meat. Add onion, garlic, cilantro, and let it simmer for about two minutes. Add red bell peppers, green olives, chicken bouillon cubes, tomato sauce, Sazon™, pigeon peas, salt and pepper. Let it simmer for about five minutes. Add the rice and water, mix it real good, bring to a boil and let the water evaporate. Mix it again, cover and cook at a low flame for about fifteen to twenty minutes.

3 cups of long grain rice
1 can pigeon peas (gandules)
2 cubes of chicken bouillon
¼ cup of green stuffed olives
1 medium chopped onion
¼ cup oil or lard
1 small can of red bell peppers
1 can tomato sauce
5½ cups boiling water
1½ pounds of pork meat cut into 1" cubes
2 cloves of garlic minced
¼ cup chopped cilantro
2 packages of Sazon™ (Caribbean seasoning found in International foods section)
salt
pepper

Large sauce pan

Beef and Pork

Stuffed Pork Chops with Apple-Raisin Dressing

Recipe from Mrs. Mylon (Ann) LeFevre
A favorite of Mylon LeFevre
Contemporary Gospel Recording Artist
Marietta, Georgia

Over medium heat, sauté apple and celery in butter for 5 minutes. Combine with remaining dressing ingredients, mixing well. With a sharp knife, cut each pork chop horizontally to form a pocket. Fill pocket with a spoonful of dressing. Brown pork chops on both sides in a small amount of shortening. Season with salt and pepper. Arrange in a baking dish and add broth. Cover and bake in oven at 350° for 1 hour or until tender. Remove pork chops to platter and thicken gravy if desired. Makes 6 servings.

6 pork chops, cut 1½" thick
shortening
½ teaspoon salt
⅛ teaspoon pepper
1 cup chicken broth

Dressing:
1 medium apple, diced
½ cup chopped celery
2 tablespoons butter
2 cups cubed raisin bread
½ teaspoon salt
1 egg beaten
¼ teaspoon poultry seasoning
¼ teaspoon marjoram leaves
½ cup chicken broth

Oven temperature 350°

Baking dish

Mylon's latest album is <u>Mylon LeFevre & Friends</u>.

Poultry

Poultry

Southern Style Chicken and Dumplings

Recipe from Charles and Laurie "Ditty" Quinn
Trinity Agapé Church, Hallandale, Florida
Jan Crouch's Sister and Brother-in-law
A favorite of the Quinn family and many friends

Put about 2 quarts of water in pot and bring to boil. Add chicken breasts and 3 to 4 boullion cubes. Cook until very tender. Debone chicken and remove excess fat and skin, put aside. Bring to boil chicken stock, put in ½ box of lasagna noodles. Turn heat to medium low, cook noodles 45 minutes until they get very tender and lose shape. Add 1 can cream of chicken soup, stir in. Add cooked chicken pieces, salt to taste, and lots of black pepper to taste. Cook on medium-low ten minutes until all mixture is hot and combined. Mixture should not be watery, but thick, creamy.

4 chicken breasts (about 3 pounds)
bouillon cubes, chicken flavor
1 can cream of chicken soup
½ box lasagna noodles
salt and pepper

6 to 8-Quart stainless steel pan with lid

Poultry

Chicken Tetrazzini

Recipe from Karen Wheaton
Gospel Recording Artist
A favorite of the Wheaton Family
Decatur, Alabama

Cook spaghetti until tender, drain. Boil chicken until tender (about 45 minutes). Reserve 1 cup of the broth. Debone chicken and cut into small pieces. Mix together chicken, pimento, onion, green pepper, mushrooms, cup of chicken broth, all soups and salt. Stir real good. Add cheese and cooked spaghetti. Mix well. Pour into baking dishes. Bake about 45 minutes on 350°in preheated oven. Remove and grate enough cheese to cover top. Place back in oven about 5 minutes until cheese melts. (If you don't want to make this much, cut the recipe in half).

2 cut-up chickens
1 cup chopped onion
½ cup chopped pimiento
½ cup chopped green pepper
1 cup chicken broth
1 large can mushrooms (drained)
2 cans cream of mushroom soup
1 can cream of chicken soup
1 can cheddar cheese soup
4 cups mild cheddar cheese (plus cheese to cover top)
1 small package of spaghetti (broken into small 2" pieces)
salt to taste

Oven temperature 350°

3 or 4 Casserole baking dishes

Karen's latest album is <u>Remembering</u>.

Lemon Dill Chicken

Recipe from Marilyn Hickey
Host of Today with Marilyn seen on TBN

Heat butter, dill, lemon juice, salt, and green onion in a large skillet over medium-low heat. Stir occasionally. Add chicken to butter mixture covering it and allowing to cook for 10 minutes. Baste it occasionally with the butter mixture inside skillet. Turn chicken and cook, covered, 10 more minutes. Arrange in warm serving dish. Pour sauce over chicken.

3 tablespoons butter
1 tablespoon chopped fresh dill
1 tablespoon fresh lemon juice
¼ teaspoon seasoned salt
1 medium green onion, thinly sliced
1 pound chicken breasts, skinned, boned and cut into pieces

Large skillet

Poultry

Chicken and Rice

Recipe from Dr. and Mrs. Lester Sumrall
Lester Sumrall Evangelistic Association
South Bend, Indiana

Soak cut-up chicken in water with 2 teaspoons lemon juice. Refrigerate for 2 hours to overnight. Stir together rice, water, sour cream, soup, and soup can of water. Sprinkle dried onion over top of mixture. Season chicken by sprinkling juice, salt, and finely chopped rosemary over it. Dust each piece with sage. Lay seasoned chicken on top of rice mixture. Drizzle honey over chicken. Bake for 1 hour or until done.

1 cut up frying chicken
2 teaspoons lemon juice
1½ cups rice
3 cups water
1 cup sour cream
1 can cream of celery soup
1 soup can of water
½ teaspoon dried minced onion
1 teaspoon rosemary
⅛ teaspoon sage
2 teaspoons honey
salt

Oven temperature 400°

Baking pan
Mixing bowl

Chicken Curry

Recipe from Sandi Barnard
A favorite recipe of Jerry Barnard
Christian Faith Center, La Mesa, California
Host of <u>Faithline</u> seen on TBN

Start preparing this dish at least 3 hours before serving. In a large stainless steel stock pot, melt the butter over medium heat. Add the spices and seasonings and brown them. Add chicken pieces and brown on all sides. Set aside. In a blender, or food processor, grind up all vegetables. Add them to the chicken. Cover and allow to simmer on low heat for at least 2 hours. Add more water as needed. Boil eggs for 10 minutes. (hint: add a dash of salt in water to assist in peeling.) Drop eggs into cold water. Peel when cooled and add to chicken and vegetable mixture. About 20 minutes before serving, thicken sauce to desired consistency by following directions on cornstarch box. Add sour cream and heat through. Serve on steamed rice (brown or white).

1 large stewing hen
6 white onions
6 green peppers
1 stalk celery
curry pepper (begin with
    2 tablespoons)
Salt and pepper
dash of sugar
cornstarch
½ pint of sour cream
2 tablespoons of butter
boiled eggs (1 for each
    person eating)

Toppings:
plump raisins
shredded coconut
sliced almonds
crushed peanuts
chutney

Large stainless steel stock pot

Sunday Chicken

Recipe from Mrs. Mike (DeAnne) Barber
A favorite of Mike Barber
Mike is host of <u>Proclaim</u> seen on TBN

Place chicken breasts in shallow baking dish, salt chicken lightly with garlic salt and use a little regular salt besides. Combine next 3 ingredients and pour over chicken. (I usually double the sauce recipe.) Bake covered for 2 hours. Serve with rice. Garnish with slices of pineapple, apricot halves, and parsley.

8 to 10 chicken breasts
1 cup Russian dressing (one bottle)
⅓ cup (small jar) apricot preserves
1 package Lipton™ onion soup (dry mix)

Oven temperature 300°

13" x 9" x 2" Baking pan

Lemon Chicken Parmesan

Recipe from Mrs. Terry (Tara) Tripp
A favorite of the LaVerne Tripp family
Gospel Songwriters and Recording Artists
Hosts of The LaVerne Tripp Family program seen on TBN

In a shallow dish, stir together egg, milk, salt, pepper, and garlic. Pound chicken breasts with mallet to flatten then, dip in egg mixture and roll in bread crumbs. In a large skillet, heat olive oil over medium heat, then cook chicken in skillet until golden brown, turning once. Drain on paper towels. Then arrange chicken in large baking dish. In a small mixing bowl, combine chicken broth, wine, and lemon juice. Pour over chicken. Sprinkle with Parmesan cheese, cover and bake at 350° for 25 minutes. Uncover and bake for 10 minutes. Garnish with lemon wedges and parsley and serve.

1 egg
1½ teaspoons milk
⅛ teaspoon salt
1 clove garlic, crushed
4 skinless boneless chicken breasts
seasoned dry bread crumbs
¼ cup olive oil
⅓ cup chicken broth
2 tablespoons white cooking wine
2 tablespoons fresh lemon juice
¼ cup grated fresh Parmesan cheese

Oven temperature 350°

Shallow mixing bowl
Large skillet

The Tripp's latest album is I'm Still Dancin'.

Javanese Dinner

Recipe from Vonette Bright
A favorite of Dr. Bill Bright
Campus Crusade for Christ
Host of New Life 2000 seen on TBN

Each item can be put in bowl and served buffet style. On each plate place: steamed rice, 2 tablespoons stewed chicken, 1 handful chow mein noodles, 1 tablespoon green onion, 1 tablespoon celery, 1 tablespoon cheese, 2 tablespoons coconut, 2 tablespoons crushed pineapple, 2 tablespoons almonds, cover with chicken gravy. To make gravy, take broth from chicken and add spices to suit your taste, such as, celery or mushrooms, soup and curry powder.

rice
chicken
chicken gravy
chow mein noodles
green onions (finely chopped)
celery (finely chopped)
cheese (grated)
shredded coconut
crushed pineapple
chopped almonds

Buffet style

Baked Chicken with Onions

Recipe from Mrs. Scotty (Lucille) Scotvold
A favorite of Scotty Scotvold
Winterhaven, California

Cover the bottom of a large baking dish with thin slices of onion. Mix in a bowl 1 can of cream of mushroom soup and ¾ can of water. Beat with egg beater and then pour over the onions. Place washed and dried pieces of chicken in the baking dish. Salt and pepper to taste. Cover with lid. Place in oven and cook for 2 to 2½ hours. 45 minutes before done, remove lid to let chicken brown (may put in potatoes to bake while chicken is cooking).

pieces of chicken (legs or breasts) with skin removed
large onion
1 can cream of mushroom soup
salt and pepper
Stove Top™ dressing (if desired) or baked potatoes

Oven temperature 375°

10" x 10" Baking dish with cover

Twenty years ago, God spoke to this precious Lutheran brother, Scotty Scotvold, just in the nick of time to hand-deliver the check that kept us from losing Ch. 40 and ultimately the network. Read the whole story in chapter 14 of I Had No Father But GOD, by Paul F. Crouch, Sr.

Chicken Mornay

Recipe from Mrs. Esther Shelton (not pictured)
(Rexella Van Impe's Mother)
A favorite of Dr. Jack and Rexella Van Impe
Hosts of Jack Van Impe Presents seen on TBN

Put one cup of instant rice in the bottom of an ungreased 9" x 12" baking dish. Place enough chicken breasts to cover the dish on top of the rice (approximately 8 skinned and boned). Top each chicken breast with a slice of Swiss cheese. Mix ½ cup of milk and one can of mushroom soup; pour over cheese and dot with butter. Sprinkle with Pepperidge Farm™ stuffing (enough to cover) and bake at 300° for 1½ hours (or until chicken is tender).

1 cup instant rice
8 chicken breasts
8 slices swiss cheese
½ cup of milk
1 can cream of mushroom
   soup
Pepperidge Farm™ stuffing

Oven temperature 300°

9" x 12" Baking dish

Poultry

Chicken Divan

Recipe from Mrs. Greg (Cathe) Laurie
A favorite of the Greg Laurie family
Harvest Christian Fellowship, Riverside, California
Host of A New Beginning seen on TBN

In baking dish arrange broccoli spears across the width of dish, flower heads facing the sides of the dish. Lay the slices of the chicken on top of the spears. Mix the condensed soup, mayonnaise, lemon juice, and curry powder. Spread across the chicken layer. Sprinkle cheddar cheese on top of soup mixture. Melt the butter in a bowl, add bread crumbs, and mix to coat them. It should still be crumbly. Sprinkle bread crumbs on top of cheese. This may be kept in the refrigerator until ready to bake. Bake at 350° until bubbly. Heat thoroughly. Bread crumbs should be toasty and cheese melted. This is a meal in itself.

2 pounds boneless chicken breasts (cooked and sliced)
1½ pounds broccoli (trim and separate into spears, steam until partly cooked)
1 can Campbell's™ cream of chicken soup
⅓ cup mayonnaise
juice of 1 lemon
2 teaspoons curry powder
¾ cup cheddar cheese, (grated)
1 teaspoon butter
¼ cup dry bread crumbs.

Oven temperature 350°

9" x 11" Baking dish

Country Captain Chicken

Recipe from Dotti Casoria
A favorite of John and Dotti Casoria
Bethany Christian Center, Loganville, Georgia
Jan Crouch's Sister and Brother-in-law

Wash chicken pieces under cold running water and pat dry with towels. Put flour, salt and pepper in plastic bag. Shake to combine thoroughly. Add 1 or 2 pieces of chicken at a time, shaking well. Heat frying pan over medium heat and then add chicken a few at a time. Brown on all sides. Put chicken in large roasting pan (chicken will not be thoroughly cooked just browned). To drippings in frying pan add onions, green and red peppers, garlic and curry powder. Sauté vegetables, stirring constantly until onion is soft. Stir in crushed tomatoes, and bring to a boil. Pour over chicken. Bake at for 400° for 1 hour. Cook rice and keep warm. Top with almonds and currants.

4 to 5 chicken breasts (split in half)
¼ cup all purpose flour
1½ teaspoons salt
½ teaspoon white pepper
4 tablespoons vegetable or olive oil
1 cup chopped onion
1 cubed green pepper
1 cubed red or yellow pepper
1 clove garlic (crushed)
1 tablespoon curry powder
2 cans (1 pound) crushed tomatoes
1 box currants
4 cups hot cooked rice
1 cup slivered almonds, toasted

Oven temperature 400°

Large paper or plastic bag
Large frying pan
Large roasting pan

Chicken with Rice

Recipe from Linda Cherry
A favorite of the Dr. Reginald B. Cherry family
Hosts of <u>Doctor</u> <u>and</u> <u>the</u> <u>Word</u> seen on TBN

Day before preparation: Boil one whole chicken, deboned, cover and refrigerate. Put chicken broth in a container and refrigerate overnight. Skim fat off top of broth. Cook 2 cups of brown rice in chicken broth (instead of water) according to package directions. In a skillet, melt the butter. Sauté celery, onion, bell pepper, parsley. Add salt and pepper, poultry seasoning and thyme. Blend well. Add skillet mixture (when celery and bell pepper are slightly tender) to rice in a large mixing bowl. Add deboned chicken. Mix well. Spray pan with a non-cholesterol, non-stick cooking spray. Spread mixture in dish. Cover with aluminum foil. Bake at 350° in preheated oven for 45 minutes. Serve with steamed broccoli and mixed green salad.

1 whole chicken, boiled and deboned (set aside)
chicken broth, refrigerated overnight, fat skimmed off
2 cups brown rice, cooked in chicken broth (fat-free method), set aside
1 stick corn oil margarine
2 stalks celery, diced
1 medium onion, diced
1 medium bell pepper, diced
2 tablespoons parsley flakes or 4 tablespoons fresh parsley
1 teaspoon light salt
½ teaspoon pepper
1 tablespoon poultry seasoning
1 teaspoon thyme

Oven temperature 350°

13" x 9" Baking dish
Large mixing bowl

Poultry

Chicken and Dumplings

Recipe from Peggy McMillan
A favorite of Terry McMillan
Gospel Recording Artist and Harmonica Virtuoso
Nashville, Tennessee

B oil, skin, and debone chicken. Keep stock and return chicken to pot. Salt and pepper to taste.

6 chicken breasts or thighs

Dumplings:
In bowl pour flour, shortening, add milk to make dough stiff. Roll out on floured board about ⅛" thickness. Cut into 1 inch squares and sprinkle generously with flour. Drop into boiling stock slowly. Cover and boil on medium heat for 8 to 10 minutes.

Dumplings:
2 cups self-rising flour
⅓ cup shortening
½ cup milk

Large pot

Chicken Croissants

Recipe from Dotti Casoria
A favorite of John and Dotti Casoria
Bethany Christian Center, Loganville, Georgia
Jan Crouch's Sister and Brother-in-law

Pull chicken off bones; place chicken on the wide end of the croissants and roll up to the small end. Bend ends and place in casserole dish. Mix milk, cheese, and soup; pour over the croissants. Bake at 350° for 40 to 45 minutes uncovered.

4 breasts of chicken
(boil until easy to peel off
skin and tear apart)
2 cans of Pillsbury™ crescent
rolls
1 cup of milk
1 cup of grated cheddar
cheese
1 can cream of chicken soup

Oven temperature 350°

Casserole dish
Saucepan

Chicken Spaghetti

Recipe from Jerry and Carolyn Savelle
A favorite of Jerry Savelle
Jerry Savelle Ministries
Crowley, Texas

Cook chicken in a pot of water and debone. Save broth and set aside 2 cups. In remaining chicken broth, cook spaghetti. Sauté in butter: onion, bell pepper, ½ cup celery. Mix together mushroom soup, chicken soup, pimentos, and cheese. Then mix spaghetti with sautéed ingredients and chicken. Pour soup mixture over spaghetti. Sprinkle ¾ cup grated cheese on top. Bake at 350° until hot and bubbly.

1 large fryer or chicken breast
1 onion, chopped
1 bell pepper chopped
½ cup celery, chopped
⅓ stick butter
1 can mushroom soup
1 can cream of chicken soup
1 medium jar pimentos
10-ounce grated Velveeta™ cheese (set aside ¾ cup)
1 can of chicken broth

Oven temperature 350°

Saucepan
Skillet
9" x 13" Casserole dish

Gavin's Turkey Loaf

Recipe from Gavin MacLeod
A favorite of Gavin and Patti MacLeod
Hosts of <u>Back On Course</u> seen on TBN

In large bowl combine turkey, onion, green pepper, parsley, eggs, garlic powder and bread crumbs. Place in loaf pan and cover with spaghetti sauce. Bake for 1 hour. Yummy.

2 pounds ground turkey breast
1 large onion, diced
1 green pepper, diced
½ bunch parsley, chopped
3 eggs
1 cup Italian bread crumbs
1 jar Paul Newman™ "Industrial Strength" spaghetti sauce

Oven temperature 350°

Loaf pan
Mixing bowl

Everyday Broccoli Cheese Chicken

Recipe from Mrs. Vern (Sandra) Jackson
A favorite of Vern Jackson
Gospel Recording Artist
Santa Ana, California

In skillet over medium heat, in hot margarine, cook chicken 10 minutes or until browned on both sides. Spoon off fat. Stir in soup, water and pepper. Heat to boiling. Add broccoli. Reduce heat to low. Cover; simmer 10 minutes or until chicken is fork-tender and broccoli is done, stirring occasionally. Makes 4 servings.

1 tablespoon margarine
4 skinless, boneless chicken
   breast halves
   (about 1 pound)
1 can Campbell's™ new
broccoli cheese soup
⅓ cup water or milk
⅛ teaspoon pepper
2 cups broccoli flowerets

Skillet

*Vern's real favorite is a Burrito Supreme with green sauce from
Taco Bell™ but they wouldn't give him the recipe!*

*Vern's latest albums are <u>Higher Than I've Ever Been</u>,
<u>O Holy Night</u>, and <u>Hello Mama</u>.*

Orange and Almond Stuffed Cornish Hens

Recipe from Dotti Casoria
A favorite of John and Dotti Casoria
Bethany Christian Center, Loganville, Georgia
Jan Crouch's Sister and Brother-in-law

Sauté onion and celery in butter in saucepan. Add orange peel, salt, sugar, poultry seasoning, 1¼ cups water, orange juice, marmalade, almonds and rice. Bring to boil; cover. Cook for 5 minutes. Stuff hens with rice mixture; place in casserole dish. Cover with foil and bake for 30 minutes at 350°. Remove foil, then bake for 45 minutes longer.

6 cornish hens
1 medium onion, chopped
1½ cup chopped celery
¼ cup butter
2 tablespoons grated orange peel
2 teaspoons salt
½ teaspoon sugar
½ teaspoon poultry seasoning
¾ cup orange juice
orange marmalade
¼ cup chopped blanched almonds
2½ cups instant rice
1¼ cups water

Oven temperature 400°

Saucepan
Casserole dish

Chicken Fricassee

Recipe from Mrs. Nicky (Gloria) Cruz
A favorite of Nicky Cruz
Colorado Springs, Colorado

Sauté cut up fryer chicken with bell pepper, onion, salt, pepper, oregano, and bay leaf. After bell pepper and onion are partially cooked (10 to 12 minutes) add wine. Cover and let simmer 45 to 50 minutes. Optional: small diced potato may be added before you cover with lid and reduce heat. Stir once or twice. Good with white rice and vegetable or salad.

1 fryer chicken, cut up
½ cup tomato paste or
¾ cup tomato sauce
¼ to ½ cup of onion and bell pepper sliced into long strips
1 bay leaf
⅛ teaspoon oregano
salt
pepper
1 garlic clove ground together with 12 to 15 capers
½ cup water
¼ cup red cooking wine
1 small potato (optional)

Deep pan

The movie The Cross And The Switchblade, starring Pat Boone and Erik Estrada, was based on the life story of Nicky Cruz!

Poultry

Orange Teriyaki Chicken with Rice Pilaf

Recipe from Evelyn Roberts
A favorite of Dr. Oral and Evelyn Roberts
Oral Roberts University, Tulsa, Oklahoma

Take 3 chicken breasts (with skin off)and wash and dry with paper towel. Place bone side down in casserole dish lying flat. Season both sides with Lawry's™ salt and powdered garlic. Pour into bottom of casserole dish ⅛ cup orange juice, ⅛ cup of white cooking wine. Spread teriyaki sauce on tops of chicken breast. Bake for 40 minutes with lid off. Baste tops with juices while cooking. Then add lid for additional cooking (15 to 20 minutes).

Rice Pilaf:

Open 1 envelope of Lipton™ chicken soup mix, dry (separate noodles from fat and powder). Mix with 2 cups of water. Add fat or chicken seasoning, let come to boil until fat is melted. In a skillet put 2 tablespoons of margarine. Melt and add noodles from envelope mix. Brown noodles and remove from fire. Add 1 cup of dry uncooked unwashed rice (I use brown rice). Let rice soak up butter in noodles. Now mix rice, noodles and soup mixture in a casserole dish, stir. Put lid on and bake at 350°. Do not stir while cooking. Cook for 1 hour.

3 chicken breasts
Lawry's™ seasoning salt
garlic powder
⅛ cup orange juice
⅛ cup white cooking wine
teriyaki sauce
1 cup rice (brown or white.)
1 envelope Lipton™ dry
**   chicken noodle soup,**
margarine

Oven temperature 350°

2 Casserole dishes

Poultry

West Coast Chicken

Recipe from Ella Smith
A favorite of Pastor Ed Smith
Trinity Christian Center of
Santa Ana, California

Combine salt, pepper, orange juice concentrate, butter, ginger and soy sauce. Grease two 11" x 7" baking pans well with vegetable oil. Place chicken in single layer in the pans; baste well with sauce. Cover; refrigerate overnight. Bake, uncovered, at 350° for about 60 minutes, basting with sauce once during cooking. Serves 8.

5 pounds chicken thighs, skinned
2 teaspoons salt
¼ teaspoon black pepper
1 cup frozen orange juice concentrate, thawed
⅓ cup butter, melted
2 teaspoons ground ginger
4 teaspoons soy sauce
vegetable oil

Oven temperature 350°

Two 11" x 7" Baking pans

Seafood and Cajun

Seafood and Cajun

Shrimp Scampi

Recipe from Carol Lawrence
Actress, Dancer and Recording Artist
Los Angeles, California

Shell and butterfly shrimp leaving the tail shell intact. Melt butter and sauté sliced garlic just until golden, then remove garlic and set aside. Sauté scampi until they turn pink. Sprinkle on parsley and add ice water. Cover tightly and immediately reduce to a simmer for 3 minutes. Sprinkle with Parmesan cheese, pepper and cover again for 1 minute. Serve immediately with hot garlic bread and enjoy.

26 to 30 scampi
large bunch of parsley
¼ pound salted butter
ground pepper
4 to 5 cloves garlic
¼ cup ice water
½ cup Parmesan cheese,
grated

Large skillet

Carol has numerous credits including a starring role in the movie "West Side Story." She is currently an active spokesperson for World Vision.

Seafood and Cajun

Salmon and Rice Dinner

Recipe from Linda Cherry
A favorite of the Dr. Reginald B. Cherry family
Hosts of Doctor and the Word seen on TBN

Cook brown rice according to package directions. Set aside. Drain and flake salmon, reserve liquid. Add enough water to reserved liquid to equal ⅓ cup. Sauté onion, celery, green pepper and curry powder in margarine. Add salmon, rice, broccoli, and reserved salmon liquid. Mix well. Season with dash of pepper. Spray baking dish with a no cholesterol, non-stick cooking spray. Spread ingredients in dish. Cover with aluminum foil. Bake for 25 to 30 minutes. Serve with steamed yellow squash and mixed green salad.

1 can salmon (7¼ ounces)
1 cup onions, chopped
½ cup celery, chopped
½ cup bell pepper, chopped
3 tablespoons corn oil
margarine
½ teaspoon curry powder
2 cups cooked brown rice
one 10-ounce package frozen chopped broccoli
fresh ground pepper

Oven temperature 350°

13" x 9" Baking dish
Aluminum foil

Steamed Fish

Recipe from Dr. and Mrs. Myles Munroe
Bahamas Faith Ministries International
Nassau, Bahamas
Host of the <u>Myles Munroe</u> program seen on TBN

Three hours before cooking dissect fish and remove all insides. Scrape all scales from fish. Scorch fish lightly and cut into two pieces. Place fish in a square baking pan. Squeeze one lime over fish especially in scorched sections. Set aside for five minutes. Sprinkle salt and pepper on scorched sections and on headsof fish. Squeeze remaining lime over fish. Set aside for three hours. Then, in a very large frying pan, pour in cooking oil. Fry fish lightly on both sides. Set fish aside. Sauté onion slightly. Add tomato paste, tomatoes and thyme. Steam for five minutes. Pour in water and bring to a boil. Add fish and cook over medium heat for 5 to 10 minutes (until gravy is thickened).

4 medium red snappers
3 teaspoons tomato paste
1 sliced ripe tomato
¾ cup water
2 limes
1 large onion, sliced
½ teaspoon leaf thyme
½ teaspoon black pepper
salt and pepper to taste

Square baking pan
Large frying pan

Seafood and Cajun

Crawfish Bisque and Roux

Recipe from Mrs. Irene Giroir (not pictured)
[Mrs. Jesse (Cathy) Duplantis' Mother]
A favorite of Jesse and Cathy Duplantis
Jesse hosts the Jesse Duplantis program seen on TBN

Clean crawfish heads, removing all membranes from head. Mix well after adding each group of ingredients. Sauté onion and celery in butter until tender. Remove from heat and add red cayenne pepper. Add eggs and stir. Then add crawfish, parsley and green onions. Add corn bread crumbs. Stuff heads with mixture. Lightly flour stuffed heads and place shell down on cookie sheet. Bake for 15 to 20 minutes or until they turn light brown. No more than 20 minutes. Set aside until roux is complete.

Roux:

Heat oil and flour. Stir constantly until flour is golden brown. Add the 1 cup onions and celery to roux. Cook until onions are light brown. Then add tomato paste and water. Let it come to a boil, reduce heat and simmer for 1 hour. After simmering add cleaned crawfish tails, parsley and green onions to roux and cook (hard boil) for 15 minutes. Gravy should be thin. Place baked stuffed heads in large baking dish. Cover heads with roux/gravy mixture. If mixture does not cover heads, add additional ½ cup water. Bake for 30 minutes or until it comes to a boil. Serve over rice.

100 crawfish heads
3 pounds boiled crawfish, (peel, de-vein, and lightly chop)
1 cup onions, chopped
1 cup celery
3 cups corn bread crumbs, or white bread crumbs
1 cup butter, not oleo
½ cup parsley
½ cup green onions
2 teaspoons red cayenne pepper
2 eggs, lightly beaten
2 cups flour

Roux:
½ cup oil
½ cup flour
4 cups water
½ cups parsley
½ cup green onions
1 cup onions
1 small can tomato paste
1 cup chopped celery
2 pounds boiled crawfish, (peel and de-vein)

Oven temperature 400°

Mixing bowl
Cookie sheet
Large baking dish
Large saucepan

154

Seafood and Cajun

Gumbo

Recipe from Rosey and Margie Grier
Actor, Gospel Recording Artist and Former NFL Player
for the Los Angeles Rams
"Are You Committed?" Ministries, Los Angeles, California

In frying pan, sauté chopped green onions (reserving green tops) and okra in the bacon fat. Add tomatoes and cook 5 to 10 minutes. Then set aside. In large pot add stock green pepper strips, green onion tops, thyme, bay leaf, salt and red pepper pod. Heat to boiling, cover and simmer 45 minutes. Add mixture from frying pan to large pot plus shrimp, crab meat, chicken, and hot links. Simmer another 45 minutes. Serve over rice in individual bowls. Serve with corn bread.

6 green onions
2 cups chopped okra
2 tablespoons bacon fat
1 cup chopped tomatoes
6 cups stock (3 chicken bouillon cubes)
4 tablespoons Worcestershire sauce,
1 clove garlic
1 pod red pepper
1 pre-cooked chicken (boiled)
1 green pepper (cut into strips)
½ teaspoon thyme
1 bay leaf
1 teaspoon salt
1 pound cooked shrimp
½ pound crab (cooked)
3 hot links (cooked and cut ½" pieces)

Frying pan
Large pot with cover

Rosey's latest album is <u>Committed</u>.

Crawfish Fettuccini

Recipe from Mrs. Jesse (Cathy) Duplantis
A favorite of Jesse Duplantis
Host of the <u>Jesse Duplantis</u> program seen on TBN

Melt oleo or butter in large pot. Add onions, celery and green peppers. Cook 10 minutes or until onion is clear. Add flour and stir well. Cover and cook 15 minutes stirring often. Add parsley and crawfish and cook for 20 minutes. Add half and half, garlic, chopped jalapeno peppers, cheese, salt and pepper. Cover and cook for 20 minutes on low heat. Add sauce to boiled fettuccini noodles in glass baking dish. Cover top with Parmesan cheese. Bake 12 to 15 minutes.

3 sticks of oleo (may be substituted with butter)
3 medium onions, chopped
3 ribs celery, chopped
2 green bell peppers, chopped
¼ cup flour
4 tablespoons of parsley
5 pounds crawfish tails
1 quart of half and half
1 pound Velveeta™ cheese
2 tablespoons of jalapeno peppers chopped
3 cloves of garlic chopped finely
salt and pepper to taste
1 pound of fettuccini noodles, boiled
Parmesan cheese

Oven temperature 350°

Large pot
Glass baking dish

Seafood Gumbo

Recipe from Candi Staton Sussewell
Gospel Recording Artist
Host of <u>Say Yes!</u> on TBN

To make a roux: brown flour and shortening together, add garlic. Cook until golden brown. Add onions, bell pepper and celery. Cook until transparent. Add shrimp and tomato sauce. Simmer for 10 minutes. Stir in water and blend well. Add all other ingredients except oysters and okra. Cook 1 hour. 20 minutes before hour is up, add okra, and 10 minutes before hour is up, add oysters. Serve in bowl with steamed rice.

6 tablespoons flour
½ cup shortening
6 cloves garlic, chopped
½ cup onion, diced
½ cup bell pepper, chopped
½ cup celery, chopped
2 pounds peeled raw shrimp, (chopped sausage or chicken pieces may be substituted)
one 8-ounce can tomato sauce
3 quarts water
1 pound crab meat
¼ bunch parsley, chopped
½ teaspoon thyme to taste
3 bay leaves
1 package of okra frozen
½ pint oysters with juice
salt and pepper to taste

Skillet
Large soup pan

Candi's latest album is <u>Standing On The Promises</u>.

Seafood and Cajun

Richard's Chicken and Sausage Jambalaya

Recipe from Richard and Lindsay Roberts
A favorite of Richard Roberts
Oral Roberts University, Tulsa, Oklahoma

Heat oil in skillet and brown chicken pieces until completely browned on all sides. Remove and set aside. In same pan add onions, scallions, green peppers, and celery. Sauté together until onions are transparent. Be sure to stir from bottom of pan to prevent sticking. Add pepper, thyme, cayenne, parsley and blend thoroughly. Remove and place in large casserole dish. Add sausage, rice, ham, tomatoes with juice, tomato sauce, and blend. Add 1 to 2 cups of water. Bring to boil. Cover, then reduce to simmer for 30 minutes. Stir occasionally. Then place uncovered casserole in 350° oven for 15 minutes. Add rice cooked to package directions.

3 tablespoons oil
4 chicken breasts
    cut into 1" pieces
1 cup chopped onions
½ cup chopped scallions
2 cloves garlic, peeled,
    minced
1 chopped green pepper
2 stalks celery, chopped
2 cups uncooked instant rice
½ teaspoon ground black
    pepper
½ teaspoon cayenne pepper
½ teaspoon thyme, dried
2 tablespoons dry parsley
½ pound smoked sausage
    (sliced in ⅛" pieces)
1 cup diced ham
    cut into 1" cubes
one 16-ounce can whole
    tomatoes in juice
1 small can tomato sauce

Oven temperature 350°

Skillet
Large casserole dish

Oyster Gumbo

Recipe from Mrs. Irene Giroir (not pictured)
[Mrs. Jesse (Cathy) Duplantis' Mother]
A favorite of Jesse and Cathy Duplantis
Jesse hosts the Jesse Duplantis program seen on TBN

To make roux: heat oil and flour, stirring constantly until dark golden brown. Add onions and brown. Reduce heat and add oysters and oyster water. Bring to a hard boil. Add remaining ingredients and let simmer for 1 hour. Salt and pepper to taste. Serve over rice.

1 cup flour
1 cup oil
1 gallon oysters (unwashed)
1 gallon oyster water, (strained) if available or regular water
4 cups onion chopped
1 cup parsley, chopped
1 cup green onion, chopped
2 tablespoons sweet basil or filé (ground sassafras leaves)
1 tablespoon pepper
salt and pepper to taste

Extra large cooking pot
4 gallon size

Seafood and Cajun

Chicken and Sausage Gumbo

Recipe from Beau and Elvina Williams
A favorite of Beau Williams
Gospel Recording Artist
Arlington, Texas

L et roux come to room temperature. In large stockpot, bring chicken broth and the water to a boil, remove from heat, and stirring strongly, blend in room temperature roux. Return pot to low heat so that the liquid bubbles gently, not boiling. Add remaining ingredients and simmer about 1 hour. Serve gumbo hot over rice.

1¼ cups roux, room
  temperature
6 cups chicken broth,
  homemade or canned
6½ cups water
3½ pounds chicken, cut
  into serving pieces
1 medium size yellow onion
1 tablespoon salt (or to taste)
1 tablespoon cayenne
1 ½ teaspoons black pepper
1½ pounds smoked
  sausages
1 cup chopped parsley
¾ cup chopped green
  onions
½ cup chopped celery
1½ teaspoons filé
  cooked rice
  (about 8 cups)

Large stock pot

Beau's latest album is <u>Love</u>.

International

International

Pastitchio

Recipe from Cheryl Kartsonakis
A Greek favorite of the Dino Kartsonakis family
Concert Pianist and Recording Artist

Sauté hamburger, drain, sauté onions and combine. Drain excess oil. Add ½ stick butter, salt, pepper, sugar, garlic, parsley, cinnamon, oregano, mint, tomato paste and 1 cup of water. Simmer for 30 minutes, remove from heat. Cook macaroni and drain, pour into large bowl. Add 1 stick butter, beaten eggs, ¼ cup cheese. Mix well. Spray or butter large pan. Add ½ cup bread crumbs, spread ½ macaroni mixture over crumbs. Cover with all of meat sauce. Mix in remaining macaroni. Cover with white sauce, then remaining cheese and bread crumbs. Dot with butter and bake for 1 hour.

White sauce:
Melt butter in pan, add cornstarch and stir until smooth. Add warm milk gradually. Stir until thickened. Add salt and cinnamon. Add beaten eggs and stir. Pour over Pastitchio. Sprinkle bread crumbs on top. Cool and cut into squares.

2 pounds hamburger
1 onion, chopped
1 garlic clove, chopped
1 tablespoon dried mint
1 tablespoon parsley, chopped
¼ teaspoon sugar
¼ teaspoon cinnamon
2 cups grated cheese, Romano
two 6-ounce cans tomato paste
2 sticks butter
1 cup water
2 pinches oregano
salt and pepper
1 pound macaroni
6 eggs, beaten
1 cup toasted bread crumbs,
**   chopped fine**

White sauce:
5 cups warm milk
4 eggs
1 stick butter
5 to 6 tablespoons cornstarch
1 teaspoon cinnamon
salt to taste

Oven temperature 350°

Large skillet, Large bowl
Baking dish

Dino's latest album is <u>Somewhere In Time</u>.

Easy Guacamole

Recipe from Mrs. Manuel (Anita) Bonilla
A favorite of the Manuel Bonilla family
Manager of Ch. 25, San Salvador, El Salvador
Hosts of Una Nueva Cancion seen on TBN

Mash avocados together, add desired salt and squeezed fresh lemon or lime juice on avocados. Mix all ingredients well. If you desire a hot taste leave in seeds of jalapeno pepper. Take out seeds if you desire a milder taste.

3 ripe avocados
1 fresh lemon or lime
salt
½ cup diced white or green onions
½ cup shredded Monterrey Jack cheese or low-fat cottage cheese
⅓ cup cilantro, diced
½ cup tomatoes, sliced
1 raw jalapeno pepper, diced
lime or lemon juice, fresh

Mixing bowl

Fresh Salsa

Recipe from Mrs. Manuel (Anita) Bonilla
A favorite of the Manuel Bonilla family
Manager of Ch. 25, San Salvador, El Salvador
Hosts of Una Nueva Cancion seen on TBN

Mix all ingredients in a bowl and add salt and pepper to desired taste. If you desire a hot taste leave all seeds in peppers. If you desire a milder taste, cut pepper in half and take out all seeds.

4 medium tomatoes, diced
1 medium onion, diced
1 jalapeno or serrano
pepper, raw, diced
1 cup cilantro, diced
salt and pepper

Medium size bowl

International

Hot Jalapeno Salsa

Recipe from Mrs. Manuel (Anita) Bonilla
A favorite of the Manuel Bonilla family
Manager of Ch. 25, San Salvador, El Salvador
Hosts of Una Nueva Cancion seen on TBN

Cook peppers in oil at medium heat, until toasted (4 to 5 minutes). Put cut onion, jalapenos with oil and salt into blender and liquefy until completely mixed. If you want this recipe very hot, keep all seeds in peppers. If you want a milder taste take out all seeds from peppers.

⅓ **cup olive oil**
4 large jalapeno peppers
½ **large white onion**
raw salt

Skillet
Blender
Mixing bowl

Tsatziki
(Salad Dressing)

Recipe from Mrs. Thanasis (Denny) Katsigiannis
A favorite recipe of Dr. Thanasis Katsigiannis
Manager of the stations in Greece
Hosts of Greek Praise the Lord

Mix the yogurt, shredded cucumbers and garlic all together. Chill and serve. This special dressing has a wonderful garlic taste that is complimented by the sweet cucumber. Some people like their Tsatziki very strong so they use a lot of garlic. Just remember, as the Tsatziki chills the garlic flavor enhances.

1 cup yogurt (plain)
2 or more cucumbers, peeled and shredded
2 or more cloves of garlic, pressed

Medium size bowl

International

Bean Salad

Recipe from Mrs. Bernard (Hazel) Roebert
A favorite of Bernard Roebert
Manager of Ch. 24, Ciskei, South Africa

Mix all ingredients together. Mix very well. Keep in refrigerator with cover on it. Marinate for a day before serving.

1 tin baked beans in tomato
    sauce
1 tin drained butter beans
1 tin drained green beans
    (cut French style)
½ cup oil
½ cup vinegar
1 cup sugar
1 chopped onion
1 chopped green pepper
4 teaspoons sweet basil
salt and pepper

Large bowl

Pepperpot
(Caribbean Recipe)

Recipe from Arthur Gilbert
Manager of Ch. 13 Nevis/St. Kitts, West Indies

Wipe all meats. Put pig's trotters or cow heel in large saucepan. Cover with water and bring to boil. Skim off fat from the surface using large spoon. Reduce heat and simmer for about 30 minutes. Skim off fat again. Add remaining meats and more water to cover, if necessary. Bring to boil again, then simmer gently, covered for 1 hour. Add remaining ingredients and continue simmering, covered for another 35 to 55 minutes, or until meats are tender. Serves 5 to 6 people.

1 kilogram (2 pounds 3 ounces) clod or brisket, cut into cubes
2 pig's trotters or 1 cow heel
250 grams (10 ounces) pickled meat
1 kilogram (2 pounds 3 ounces) oxtail, cut into joints
2 red peppers, deseeded and chopped
3 cloves
25 ml spoon (1½ tablespoons) sugar
1 piece dried orange or lemon peel, about 2.5 centimeters (1") long
1 piece cinnamon stick, about 2.5 centimeters (1") long
250 ml (½ pint) cassareep
salt to taste

Large saucepan with lid

Steak and Onions

Recipe from Jon Karner
TBN's Liaison to Russia and Translator
Torrance, California
A favorite of the Russian people

Cut the meat into ⅓" thick strips. Pound the meat on both sides until tender. Coat the meat with flour and season with salt and pepper. Fry the meat in hot margarine on both sides until golden brown. Sauté the sliced onions in hot margarine until golden brown. Place a layer of steak in the pressure cooker and cover with a layer of onions. Top onions with sour cream. Place another layer of steak in the pressure cooker and cover again with onions and sour cream. Repeat this until all steak and onions are placed in the pressure cooker. Pour the boiling water over the ingredients and under pressure on low temperature, boil twenty minutes. Serve with boiled potatoes and steamed vegetables.

2 pounds steak
¼ cup margarine
6 onions, sliced
dash of salt and pepper
flour to coat the meat
1 to 2 cups boiling water
sour cream

Frying pan
Pressure cooker

Eggplant Stuffed and Rolled

Recipe from Dom DeLuise
Actor/Comedian
Los Angeles, California

Wash eggplants, remove stems, peel, and slice lengthwise. Dredge eggplant in flour. Dip into beaten egg and fry until golden brown. Pat dry with paper towels. Place a slice of mozzarella in the middle of each eggplant slice. Add a scoop of ricotta. Roll up eggplant slices and place eggplant rolls, seam side down, in greased shallow baking pan and top with a little Marinara sauce. Bake for 15 to 30 minutes. If desired, garnish with chopped parsley, and grated cheese. Great with pasta on the side.

2 medium eggplants
flour for dredging
2 eggs, beaten
olive oil
½ pound sliced mozzarella
1 pound ricotta mixed with
    1 tablespoon of finely
    chopped parsley
2 cups marinara sauce
grated cheese (if desired)

Oven temperature 350°

Skillet
Shallow baking pan

International

Patti's World Class Eggplant

Recipe from Patti MacLeod
A favorite of Gavin MacLeod
Hosts of <u>Back</u> <u>On</u> <u>Course</u> seen on TBN

Peel eggplant and slice into ½" round pieces. Soak in very salty water for an hour. This is to remove the acid from the eggplant. The water will turn light brown, pour off. Then in two dishes place beaten eggs in one and bread crumbs in other. In frying pan heat olive oil about ½" deep on medium heat. It's important to keep the oil at just the right temperature. Do not get it too hot so that it smokes. Dip each slice of eggplant first into the beaten eggs and then into the bread crumbs. Then place into the frying pan cooking one side first and then the other, until golden brown. Add more olive oil as needed. Having already poured a light layer of spaghetti sauce into the bottom of the deep casserole dish, then lay eggplant slices into the bottom of the dish completely covering the bottom of dish. Then add more sauce, a generous dab of ricotta cheese and mozzarella cheese. Repeat this layer until your casserole dish is filled or you have used all the eggplant. Top with a layer of sauce and sprinkle Parmesan cheese. Bake uncovered for 45 minutes to 1 hour. This dish may be stored uncooked and covered in refrigerator until the next day. Bon Appetite!

2 large eggplants
3 eggs
Italian bread crumbs
olive oil
1 pint ricotta cheese
½ pound shredded mozzarella cheese
Parmesan cheese
spaghetti sauce

Oven temperature 325°

1 Large deep rectangular casserole dish
2 Pie type plates
1 Large frying pan

172

Sugo All' Amatriciana (Pasta Sauce)

Recipe from Nora Hall
A favorite of Chuck Hall
European Regional Representatives of TBNE
Hosts of Italian <u>Praise</u> <u>the</u> <u>Lord</u>

Heat oil and add bacon, cook over high heat, stirring constantly with a wooden spoon until browned and well done. Remove bacon from oil and place where it will remain warm. Add chopped onions and chili pepper to the oil. Cook until onions begin to brown slightly. Add tomatoes (they must be thick and not watery). Salt and cook on medium heat for 15 minutes stirring frequently. Add cooked bacon pieces to the sauce and stir. Cook and drain pasta "al dente" (firm, not mushy). Add drained pasta to the sauce, mix well and cook until pasta is desired texture. Put pasta in serving bowls and grate Pecorino cheese over each bowl. Serve hot.

½ pound lean smoked bacon (pancetta) cut in ½" squares
1 large can 28-ounce Italian style tomatoes, chopped
½ medium sized onion, chopped finely
1 or 2 small red chili peppers (dry) use whole not chopped
5 tablespoons extra virgin olive oil
Pecorino cheese (Romano)
salt
1 pound pasta bucatini or large spaghetti

Large deep skillet

Meat and Cheese Manicotti

Recipe from Joni Parsley
A favorite of Rod Parsley
World Harvest Church, Columbus, Ohio
Host of <u>Breakthrough</u> seen on TBN

Combine drained ground beef, tomato sauces, onions, spices, and Parmesan cheese and cook in large kettle on low heat for 1 hour. Combine cheeses and spices for filling. Mix thoroughly with spoon. Bring 4 quarts of water to a boil. Add pasta slowly and stir. Return to a boil for 8 minutes (uncovered). Drain. Cool in single layers on wax paper to avoid pasta sticking together. Spread a thin layer of sauce on bottom of 13" x 9" baking pan. Spoon cheese filling into manicotti and place in single layer over sauce. Cover layer with remaining sauce and any extra mozzarella or Parmesan cheese. Cover with aluminum foil, bake for 40 minutes. Remove foil and bake for 15 minutes.

1 pound lean ground beef, (cooked and drained)
one 15-ounce can Italian stewed tomatoes
1 medium bell pepper, optional
¼ cup grated Parmesan cheese
one 28-ounce can tomato sauce
one 15-ounce can Italian tomato sauce
1 medium sized onion, chopped
½ teaspoon salt and pepper
¼ teaspoon oregano and garlic salt
one 8-ounce box manicotti uncooked

Filling:
2 cups cottage cheese
½ cup shredded Parmesan cheese
2 cups mozzarella cheese
¼ teaspoon salt and pepper

Oven temperature 350°

Large kettle
5-Quart saucepan
Wax paper
13" x 9" Baking pan

Paglia and Fieno
(Straw and Hay)

Recipe from Michelle Corral
Director of Breath of the Spirit International
Ministries and West Coast Conference on the Holy
Spirit and Christian Unity, Orange, California

Mix by hand, all ingredients (you may add more or less according to your party). Be sure there is at least 1½ cups water in the pan. Scoop meatballs with a extra large ice cream scoop (they should be the size of a small baseball). Place them on aluminum tray, and bake at least 40 minutes.

Sauce:
In a large pot, brown slightly tomato paste, 4 cloves garlic and onion. Add puree, mix well with paste. Add tomatoes with juice, break up the tomatoes to desired consistency. Then add parsley, oregano, basil, garlic powder and salt. Stir well, keep stirring on low flame. After 1 hour, ½ cup water, ½ cup of sugar, can be added to make the sauce unbelievably Sicilian. After meatballs are finished add ½ of the juice from them to the sauce to give it a meat flavor.

6 pounds ground beef
2 cups grated Parmesan or Romano cheese
2½ cups seasoned Progresso™ bread crumbs
7 fresh eggs
½ cup fresh parsley (finely chopped)
½ tablespoon garlic powder or 1 tablespoon garlic salt
½ teaspoon table salt
4 cups water (may add a little more)

Sauce:
1 can Contadina™ tomato paste
¼ cup sweet basil (finely chopped)
¼ cup onion (chopped)
4 cloves garlic (chopped)
¼ cup fresh parsley (chopped)
1 tablespoon garlic powder
hint of oregano
2 large cans tomato puree
1 can of whole peeled Progresso™ tomatoes with basil
1 tablespoon of salt
½ cup sugar (optional)

Oven temperature 400°

Ice cream scoop
Flat aluminum pan
Large pot for sauce

International

Lasagna

Recipe from Mrs. J. Don (Gwen) George
A favorite of J. Don George and their daughter Valerie
Calvary Temple, Irving, Texas

Simmer meat, garlic, seasoning, salt, tomato sauce. Cook noodles in large saucepan. Mix cottage cheese, Parmesan cheese, eggs, salt and pepper. First layer noodles in baking dish, then layer cottage cheese mixture. Third layer should be meat sauce. Repeat layers again. Place mozzarella cheese on top. Bake for 30 minutes, let stand for 10 minutes then serve.

1 pound lean hamburger
1 clove garlic
1 tablespoon Italian seasoning
1½ teaspoons salt
2 cans tomato sauce
6 large lasagna noodles
1 small carton cottage cheese
½ cup Parmesan cheese
2 eggs
1 teaspoon salt and pepper
½ pound mozzarella cheese,
    sliced thin

Oven temperature 375°

8" x 11" Baking dish
Saucepan
Skillet

Dom's Meatballs

Recipe from Dom DeLuise
Actor and Comedian
Los Angeles, California

Place all ingredients in large bowl and mix thoroughly. Let stand ½ hour. Shape into medium size meatballs. Fry gently in olive oil until lightly browned, or place on foil on cookie sheet and bake for 30 minutes. Place in your own hot spaghetti sauce and cook for 1 hour over medium heat

2 pounds ground beef
½ pound ground pork
2 cups Italian flavored bread crumbs
4 eggs
1 cup milk
1 cup fresh parsley, chopped
½ cup grated cheese
1 tablespoon olive oil
2 garlic cloves, chopped very fine
1 onion, minced
½ cup pignoli (pine nuts) (optional)

Oven temperature 350°

Frying pan or cookie sheet
Large mixing bowl

177

Paglia and Fieno (Straw and Hay)

Recipe from Nora Hall
A favorite of Chuck Hall
European Regional Representatives of TBNE
Hosts of Italian <u>Praise</u> <u>the</u> <u>Lord</u>

Fry bacon until brown, melt butter in skillet and add mushrooms. Sauté mushrooms lightly. Then add peas. Then add cream and cook on medium heat for 2 to 3 minutes. stirring constantly. Have pasta cooking in abundantly salted boiling water (both noodles together) until texture is firm but not hard. Only about 3 minutes if pasta is fresh. Drain pasta and add immediately to sauce that is cooking. Mix well in skillet. Cook for 2 to 3 minutes then serve and eat immediately. Sprinkle Parmesan cheese over each serving.

½ **pound lean smoked bacon (pancetta) cut in ½" squares**
¼ **pound butter**
½ **pint heavy cream**
2½ **cups sliced mushrooms**
1 **cup firmly cooked peas**
½ **pound fettuccine, white**
½ **pound fettuccine, green**
½ **cup Parmesan (Parmigiana) cheese, freshly grated**

Large skillet

Fettuccini Alfredo

Recipe from Mrs. Jay (Pam) Sekulow
A favorite of Jay, Jordan, and Logan Sekulow
Christian Advocates Serving Evangelism, Atlanta, Georgia
Host of A Call to Action seen on TBN

Cook fettuccini in salted boiling water until tender, about 10 minutes. Drain water, add grated cheese, butter and cream. Mix thoroughly, serve.

1 pound fresh fettuccini noodles
6 tablespoons butter
1 cup heavy cream (room temperature)
¾ cup fresh grated Parmesan cheese

Saucepan

179

Italian Chicken

Recipe from Kathy Hayes
A favorite of Mike and Kathy Hayes
Covenant Church, Carrollton, Texas

Wash all chicken pieces. Melt butter in bottom of pans and place part of onion rings in butter. Sprinkle a light coat of each seasoning on mixture. Dip chicken pieces in butter, turn over and place remainder of onion on top and lightly season again with all the listed seasonings. Cover with foil and bake 30 to 40 minutes. Remove from oven and remove foil. Cover the chicken with mushrooms. Leave the foil off and bake 15 minutes until brown. Take out again and cover with mozzarella cheese. Cover with foil and turn oven down considerably. This is a very flexible dish, especially if your guests are late. This dish goes well with angel hair pasta.

6 boneless skinless chicken breasts
6 chicken thighs
2 sticks butter
4 onions, sliced round
lemon pepper
oregano
garlic salt
2 large cans of mushrooms
3 cups grated mozzarella

Oven temperature 350°

Two 9" x 12" baking dishes
Aluminum foil

Spaghetti and Meat Sauce

Recipe from Cindy Way
A favorite of Del Way
Gospel Recording Artist and Pastor of
Calvary Temple, Kerrville, Texas

Brown ground beef. Add onion, bell pepper, celery, and dry ingredients. Cook until they are tender. Transfer to large pot and add remaining ingredients and cook for 2 hours on low heat. Boil spaghetti noodles (with a little butter to prevent sticking) until tender, drain and add to sauce mixture. Serve with tossed salad and garlic bread.

2 pounds ground beef
three 8-ounce Contadina™ tomato sauce
one 6-ounce Contadina™ tomato paste
one 16-ounce whole tomatoes
4 celery stalks (chopped)
1 onion (chopped)
1 bell pepper (chopped)
1 small can mushrooms (optional)
1 package Skinner™ vermicelli noodles
2 teaspoons oregano
2 teaspoons garlic powder
salt and pepper to taste

Skillet
Saucepan
Large pot

Del's latest album is You'll Never Be The Same.

Pasta e Fagioli

Recipe from Carol Lawrence
Actress, Dancer and Recording Artist
Los Angeles, California

Sauté onions in drippings until wilted. Add tomato paste, salt, pepper, parsley, basil and simmer for 10 minutes. Add strained beans and simmer 5 minutes or more. In separate pan, boil shells and leave in water. Add tomato mixture to shells that have been left in water. Serve with grated Parmesan cheese.

½ pound pasta shells
2 teaspoons drippings from
** southern fried chicken**
1 small can tomato paste
1 regular can dark kidney
** beans or 1 regular can**
** white beans**
1 big onion, chopped
salt, pepper, parsley and basil
** to taste**
Parmesan cheese, grated

Deep saucepan
Skillet

Carol has numerous credits including a starring role in the movie
"West Side Story." She is currently an active spokesperson for World Vision.

Giovanni's Italian Meat Sauce

Recipe from Dr. John DeSarno Casoria
A favorite of John and Dotti and all of the Casoria clan
Bethany Christian Center, Loganville, Georgia
Jan Crouch's Sister and Brother-in-law

Mix together all ingredients in large pot (preferably stainless steel). Bring to rapid boil, stirring frequently, then reduce heat to a simmer. Continue to stir as often as needed to keep sauce from sticking to bottom of pot. Cook at very low boiling point for 4 to 6 hours, stirring occasionally. In frying pan, put hamburger meat. Cook on medium heat, mashing with fork until well done. Drain excess fat and add to marinara sauce. Stir well, serve over pasta of your choice.

4 cans whole peeled tomatoes
2 cans tomato paste
1 large can tomato juice
½ cup oregano
1 tablespoon salt
1 tablespoon garlic salt
½ cup grated Romano
   or Parmesan cheese
½ green pepper, left uncut

Optional:
1 pound choice hamburger
   meat

Large pot
Skillet

Chicken and Rice

Recipe from Jonas Gonzalez, Jr. (not pictured)
and Jonas Gonzalez, Sr.
Station Managers of Ch. 23 San José, Costa Rica
A favorite Latin American recipe

Cook the chicken breasts in the 2 cups of water, until done. Set aside and cool. When they are cold, chop them in pieces. Fry the onion and the red pepper in oil. Stir in the rice, chicken and the consommé. Cover and cook on low heat until done.

2 chicken breasts
½ teaspoon salt
¼ teaspoon black pepper
2 cups water

For Rice:
2 cups rice
1 tablespoon onion, chopped
1 tablespoon red pepper, chopped
1 teaspoon salt

Skillet

Easy Lasagna

Recipe from Chris Holloway
Gospel Recording Artist
Houston, Texas

Brown meat slowly (spoon off excess fat). Add garlic, basil, oregano, parsley flakes, tomatoes, tomato paste, water, salt and pepper. Simmer uncovered for 1 hour. Stir often. Cook noodles as directed on package. In large bowl combine eggs, ricotta and Parmesan cheese. Stir thoroughly. Layer half of noodles in pan. Spread half of ricotta filling, half the mozzarella cheese and half of the meat sauce. Repeat second layer with remaining ingredients. Bake at 350° for 30 minutes.

1 pound lean ground beef
1 clove garlic
1 teaspoon basil
½ teaspoon oregano
1 large can whole tomatoes
two 6-ounce cans tomato paste
10 ounces lasagna noodles
2 eggs
1 cup water
3 cups ricotta cheese
½ cup Parmesan cheese
2 tablespoons parsley flakes
1 teaspoon salt
½ teaspoon black pepper
1 pound mozzarella cheese

Oven temperature 350°

13" x 9" Baking pan
Large skillet
Large mixing bowl

Chris' latest album is <u>The Love Of God</u>.

Lindsay's Spaghetti Sauce

Recipe from Lindsay Roberts
A favorite of the Richard Roberts family
Oral Roberts University, Tulsa, Oklahoma

In large skillet, brown the ground beef and onions until the meat is completely browned. Drain off all the fat. Transfer meat and onions to a large 8 to 10-quart pot. Add tomato paste, tomato sauce, and 2 cans water. Stir over low heat until all are dissolved together and add garlic, oregano, sugar and pepper. Let this simmer on low for at least 4 hours, stirring occasionally. Be sure not to get it too hot as it will burn quickly. Then taste for seasoning, if it needs more flavor, add a little more garlic, oregano, and/or salt. Add only one at a time and taste. Be sure you wait 4 hours to adjust the seasoning. It will get stronger as it simmers. Then, if it's a little "bitter" add 1or 2 teaspoons sugar and stir. Be sure to skim off any fat that rises to the top. If you like mushrooms, add them about 15 minutes before serving.

2 pounds lean ground beef
1 medium onion (coarsely chopped)
2 whole garlic cloves (pressed through garlic press)
1½ tablespoons ground oregano
1½ to 2 teaspoons sugar
two 12-ounce cans tomato sauce
two 12-ounce cans tomato paste
2 to 3 cans water (use the tomato cans)
¼ teaspoons coarse ground pepper
one 8-ounce can mushrooms or fresh chopped mushrooms

Large skillet
8 to 10-Quart pot

Island Vegetables

Recipe from Dr. and Mrs. Myles Munroe
Bahamas Faith Ministries International
Nassau, Bahamas
Host of the <u>Myles Munroe</u> program seen on TBN

Sauté onion, sweet pepper, celery and tomatoes in vegetable oil. In separate saucepan, place salt beef with enough water to cover and bring to a boil. Discard all but 3 tablespoons beef water. Add beef (including water) to ingredients in pot. Add peas and remaining seasonings. Add tomato paste and water. Mix well. Bring water to a boil. Wash rice and add to boiling water. Stir and reduce heat to very low flame. Cook for 40 to 50 minutes or until done.

3 cups rice
4 cups water
2 tablespoons vegetable oil
1½ medium onions
½ medium sweet pepper
2 ripe tomatoes
2 cups green peas, boiled
1 tablespoon seasoned salt
¼ pound salt beef
1 celery stalk

Skillet
Saucepan
Medium size pot

International

Stewed Chicken
with Pineapple Sauce

Recipe from Nora Lam
Missionary Evangelist to China
Host of Chinese Praise the Lord

Clean chicken and soak with soy sauce and wine for 30 minutes. Deep fry chicken in the hot oil until it becomes golden brown. Remove the chicken and drain off oil from frying pan. Put back only 3 tablespoons oil in pan, and stir fry the onions. Add the remaining soy sauce and pineapple juice. Add the chicken, then add cold water, cover with lid. Stew at low heat about 30 minutes to 1 hour, until chicken is done. Remove the chicken and cut into 2" pieces. Add pineapple into the pan, cook with the chicken liquid for 3 minutes (low heat). Add cornstarch paste and sesame oil, stir well. Pour the sauce over the chicken, with parsley leaves on top for decoration.

1 whole chicken
   (about 2 pounds)
⅔ can pineapple diced
½ onion diced
½ can pineapple juice
5 parsley leaves
5 tablespoons soy sauce
1 tablespoon wine
2½ cups cold water
1 tablespoon cornstarch
   (make paste)
1 tablespoon cold water
1 teaspoon sesame oil
5 cups oil

Large frying pan

TBN's award-winning, premier movie, "China Cry"
was based on the life story of Nora Lam.

Stir Fried Rice

Recipe from Nora Lam
Missionary Evangelist to China
Host of Chinese Praise the Lord

Heat 2 tablespoons oil in pan. Pour in the beaten eggs and stir fry quickly until eggs are in tiny pieces. Remove from pan. Heat another 3 tablespoons oil, stir fry shrimp and ham, add green peas , fry about 1 minute and remove from pan. Heat another 3 tablespoons oil in same frying pan, fry the onion and cooked rice, mix well. Sprinkle salt on top. Reduce heat and stir until rice is thoroughly heated, then add all ingredients together. Mix well and serve.

½ cup small shrimp, cooked or fresh
½ cup roast pork or ham, diced
2 eggs
2 tablespoons green peas
1 tablespoon raisins, optional
2 tablespoons chopped green onions
6 cups cooked rice
2 teaspoons salt
8 tablespoons oil

Large frying pan

TBN's award-winning, premier movie, "China Cry" was based on the life story of Nora Lam.

Chicken Enchiladas

Recipe from Sharon White (Mrs. Ricky Skaggs)
A favorite of Ricky Skaggs
Country and Gospel Recording Artist
Nashville, Tennessee

Combine first 5 ingredients in a large mixing bowl. Add half a can of cream of mushroom soup. Melt 1 tablespoon butter in the bottom of a 13" x 9" x 2" baking dish. Fill the tortillas with the chicken mixture; sprinkle with hot sauce to taste and roll up. Place seam side down in the prepared baking dish. Melt 2 tablespoons butter and 1½ cans of soup together in a saucepan. Pour over enchiladas and bake, uncovered, for 30 minutes in a 350° oven. Enchiladas should be golden brown. Garnish with sour cream and avocado slices. Serve with rice and beans. Makes 10 enchiladas.

4 large chicken breasts, cooked, deboned and diced
3 cups Monterey Jack cheese, grated (may use cheese with jalapeno peppers)
1 large onion, diced
one 4-ounce can diced green chilies
1 cup sour cream
3 tablespoons butter
2 cans cream of mushroom soup
hot sauce to taste (from a jar or can)
10 flour tortillas (oven warmed)
avocados (optional)

Oven temperature 350°

Large mixing bowl
13" x 9" x 2" Baking dish
Saucepan

Enchiladas

Recipe from Dr. Donald Whitaker
A favorite of Don and Helen Whitaker
Host of Calling Dr. Whitaker seen on TBN

B lend the pinto beans, ⅔ cup spaghetti sauce and ⅓ salsa together coarsely in the blender. Transfer to a bowl and add the rice, 1 tablespoon vegetable broth seasoning and onions. Put 2 heaping tablespoons of the mixture into each corn tortilla and roll up. Place side by side in the baking dish. Make sure dish is sprayed with PAM™ or other non-stick cooking spray. In a bowl mix ½ cup salsa with the ¼ cup spaghetti sauce and 1 tablespoon vegetable broth seasoning. Pour evenly over the rolled tortillas. Sprinkle over the top with Parmesan cheese. Cover with foil and seal. Bake for 30 minutes.

1 cup cooked pinto beans
⅔ cup unsalted spaghetti sauce
¼ cup unsalted spaghetti sauce
⅓ cup salsa (mild to hot)
¼ cup salsa (mild to hot)
1 cup cooked brown rice
1 tablespoon vegetable broth seasoning
½ cup chopped onions
Parmesan cheese
corn tortillas

Oven temperature 350°

6" x 10" Pyrex™ baking pan

International

Lemon Chicken with Potatoes

Recipe from Mama Katsigiannis (not pictured)
A favorite recipe of Thanasis and Denny Katsigiannis
Manager of the stations in Greece
Hosts of Greek <u>Praise the Lord</u>

Wash chicken thoroughly. Sprinkle with oregano, salt and pepper. Place in baking pan. Add potatoes spreading out evenly around chicken. Sprinkle salt, pepper and oregano on potatoes mixing thoroughly. In bowl mix lemon juice and olive oil. Pour this mixture evenly over potatoes and chicken. Add enough water to prevent sticking but do not completely cover all the potatoes. It might take a few times to know exactly the amount because it varies. Additional water may be necessary during baking. Bake 1½ hours basting 3 or 4 times during cooking.

1 roasting chicken, whole
6 to 8 potatoes, peeled and
**   quartered**
1 to 2 tablespoons oregano
2 to 4 lemons, juice only
½ cup olive oil
water
salt and pepper to taste

Oven temperature 375°

Baking pan
Mixing bowl

Zharkoye
(Beef and Potato Stew)

Recipe from Jon Karner
TBN's Liaison to Russia and Translator
Torrance, California
A favorite of the Russian people

Wash and peel potatoes. Cut into 4 pieces. Brown potatoes in 2 tablespoons of the oil, for about 10 minutes. Set aside. Wash and chop onions. Sauté in 1 tablespoon oil. When brown, add tomato juice and flour and stir until flour is well mixed. Set aside. Cut meat in small cubes. Rub in salt and pepper. In a large frying pan, brown the meat in remaining oil. Pour beef broth over browned meat. Add salt and pepper and stew for 40 to 50 minutes until tender. Skim off excess fat. Into a dutch oven or a large clay pot, transfer meat, broth, potatoes, onion mixture, crushed garlic, dill, parsley, and bay leaves. Cover and place in a 350° oven for 30 minutes. Meat is brown and soft when ready. Serve in big bowls.

2 pounds meat (beef)
16 small potatoes
5 onions
2 tablespoons flour
4 tablespoons tomato juice
5 tablespoons olive oil
1 can beef or chicken broth
2 cloves fresh garlic, crushed
salt
pepper
dill
parsley
bay leaves

Oven temperature 350°

Dutch oven or large clay pot

Bobotie
(South African dish)

Recipe from Mrs. Bernard (Hazel) Roebert
A favorite of Bernard Roebert
Manager of Ch. 24, Ciskei, South Africa

Fry the onions in the margarine and oil and add the curry and turmeric. Remove from heat and add jam or chutney, sugar, salt and pepper, fruit, lemon peel and vinegar/lemon juice. Combine the bread and meat and add to the curry mixture. Mix well and lastly add the almonds. Pour into oven proof dish and bake for 45 minutes. Add a few orange, lemon, or bay leaves before putting into the oven. Remove from oven. Pour the two beaten eggs, ½ cup milk and salt and pepper over the meat. Return to the oven and bake for another 30 to 35 minutes until the egg is done. Serve with yellow rice and raisins (1 cup rice cooked with 1 teaspoon turmeric and raisins to taste). Top with apricot jam or fruit chutney.

2 onions, sliced
margarine
oil
2 tablespoons curry powder
1 tablespoon apricot jam or
**   chutney**
2 tablespoons sugar
2 teaspoons salt
¼ cup seedless raisins
¼ cup dried sliced peaches
1 small apple sliced
½ teaspoon pepper
1 teaspoon grated lemon peel
2 teaspoons turmeric
¼ cup vinegar or lemon juice
2 pounds beef, minced
2 slices bread soaked in
**   ⅓ cup milk**
2 eggs
a few almonds
½ cup milk
orange, lemon, or bay leaves

Oven temperature 300°
Big saucepan
12" x 12" Baking dish

Velvet Pudding

Recipe from Mrs. Bernard (Hazel) Roebert
A favorite of Bernard Roebert
Manager of Ch. 24, Ciskei, South Africa

B eat egg whites stiffly, add sugar and beat well, then set aside. Mix maizina (cornstarch), sugar, yolks, vanilla essence together with some cold milk. Bring to boil 1 pint milk and butter. Thicken with the maizina mixture. Pour into pie dish and spread youngberry jam over top. Cover youngberry jam with the stiffly beaten egg whites. Bake at 350° until golden brown.

2 heaped tablespoons maizina (cornstarch)
2 cups sugar
3 egg yolks
1 pint of milk
1 tablespoon butter
1 teaspoon vanilla essence
youngberry jam
3 egg whites
3 tablespoons sugar

Oven temperature 350°

12" x 8" Pyrex™ dish
or round Pyrex™ dish

International

Okra "A La Egyptian"

Recipe from Hazel Crouch
A favorite of Dr. Philip Crouch
Manager Ch. 58, Irving, Texas, and Pastor of
Trinity Christian Center Church of Irving, Texas

Brown ground beef, drain fat, if any. Remove from pan. Lightly brown onion and green pepper in one tablespoon oil. Garlic should be added at this time, either chopped fine or pressed through garlic press. Return beef to skillet. Add the sauces and water with salt and pepper as desired. Let simmer uncovered about half an hour, or until sauce begins to thicken. Add okra, bit of salt, cover, let simmer until okra is tender. Remove lid if sauce is too thick. Do not overcook okra. Serve over brown rice. Should be served with sesame dip and pita bread.

okra, fresh baby or
    frozen whole baby okra
**1 pound extra lean ground
    beef**
1 onion, chopped
½ green onion , chopped
1 can tomato paste
1 can water
1 can tomato sauce
1 or 2 cloves garlic, if desired
salt to taste

Large skillet with lid

Philip and Hazel served as Missionaries to Egypt for 20 years.

Bread Pudding

*Recipe from Jonas Gonzalez, Jr. (not pictured)
and Jonas Gonzalez, Sr.*
Station Managers of Ch. 23 San José, Costa Rica
A favorite Latin American recipe

The bread should be in little pieces. It can be cut with a knife or torn with your hands. Put it in a big bowl and add the milk so the bread will get soaked. Then add the condensed milk and the melted butter. combine everything and add the vanilla and raisins last. Mix everything and put into greased pan. Bake for 45 minutes or until done.

2 bread loaves
1 cup sugar
2 liters milk
1 can condensed milk
1 cup raw raisins
2 tablespoons of melted margarine
1 teaspoon vanilla extract

Oven temperature 375°

13" x 9" Greased pan
Large bowl

International

Melk Tert

Recipe from Mrs. Bernard (Hazel) Roebert
A favorite of Bernard Roebert
Manager of Ch. 24, Ciskei, South Africa

Cream butter and sugar, and add slightly beaten egg. Add sifted flour, baking powder and salt. Press pastry into pie plate.

6 tablespoons flour
3 tablespoons butter
1 egg
1½ tablespoons sugar
1½ teaspoons baking powder
pinch of salt

Filling for pastry:
Mix together maizina (cornstarch), flour, sugar, salt, with some cold milk. Beat eggs and vanilla essence together. Bring to boil 1 pint of milk and lump of butter, thicken with your mixed together maizina, flour etc. Remove from stove and add your beaten eggs and vanilla essence. Pour into pastry lined plate and bake in oven until golden brown. Take out and sprinkle well with cinnamon.

Filling for pastry:
1 pint milk
1 heaped tablespoon maizina
    (cornstarch)
1 heaped tablespoon flour
½ cup sugar
pinch of salt
lump of butter
2 eggs
1 teaspoon vanilla essence

Oven temperature 375°

1" x 10" pie plate

New Mexico Style Sopapillas

Recipe from Julie Arguinzoni
A favorite of Sonny Arguinzoni
Victory Outreach
La Puente, California

Thoroughly mix dry ingredients, then add shortening and mix until it is thoroughly dissolved. Slowly add one cup of warm water and knead until smooth. Your dough should then be about the consistency of pie dough or possibly a little stiffer. Cover the dough with a damp cloth and let rise for 2 hours. For a more consistent rise, refrigerate the dough overnight then allow it to warm to room temperature prior to cooking.

4 cups flour
¾ teaspoons salt
2 teaspoons baking powder
1 tablespoon shortening
1 cup warm water

Frying temperature 425°

Deep fryer

For cooking:

Roll the dough out very thin, between ¹⁄₁₆" and ¹⁄₃₂" then cut the dough into rectangular strips of about 3" x 4". Cook in a deep pan in at least ½" to ¾" of very hot shortening or vegetable oil, about 425°. Then cook as you would doughnuts; the sopapillas will begin to puff up as they cook. Remove them as they turn slightly golden. Serve hot with butter and or honey.

Note:

If the sopapillas do not puff up as they should, it is possible that either the cooking oil was not hot enough, the dough had not risen for long enough, or the dough was rolled too thick.

International

Fluffy Pudding

Recipe from Jon Karner
TBN's Liaison to Russia and Translator
Torrance, California
A favorite of the Estonian people

Beat egg whites until stiff, set aside. Cream the egg yolks with the sugar. Add the flour. Bring the milk to a boil. Add a small part of the warm milk to the egg yolk mixture. Mix. Then add the yolk mixture to the rest of the hot milk. Stir the milk mixture until it thickens. Add the vanilla and salt. Add the whipped egg whites. Serve cold with strawberries.

3 cups milk
4 eggs, separated
⅔ cup sugar
3 tablespoons flour
1 teaspoon vanilla
dash of salt

Desserts

Desserts

Pecan Tassies

Recipe from Mrs. Mike (DeAnne) Barber
A favorite of Mike Barber
Host of <u>Proclaim</u> seen on TBN

L et cream cheese and ½ cup butter soften at room temperature. Blend together. Stir in flour and chill about 1 hour. Shape in 2 dozen 1" balls. Place in ungreased 1¾" muffin pan. Press dough against bottoms and sides.

Pecan Filling:

Beat together egg, brown sugar, butter, vanilla and salt just until smooth. Divide half the pecans among pastry-lined pans. Add egg mixture and top with remaining pecans. Bake in oven for 25 minutes or until filling is set. Cool and remove from pans. Makes 2 dozen.

Cheese Pastry:
one 3-ounce package cream
   cheese
½ cup butter
1 cup sifted all-purpose flour

Pecan Filling:
1 egg
¾ cup brown sugar
1 tablespoon soft butter
1 teaspoon vanilla
dash salt
⅔ cup chopped pecans

Oven temperature 325°

1¾" Muffin pan

Peanut Butter Candy

Recipe from Judy Lindberg McFarland
Nutritionist
Torrance, California
Our children's favorite candy!

Mix peanut butter and add in powdered milk a little at a time, until smooth (the amount of powdered milk depends on the dryness of the peanut butter). Add honey and seed mixture. the mix should be the consistency of bread dough. Wrap in Saran Wrap™ or wax paper, chill and slice.

2 pounds crunchy peanut butter (non-hydrogenated, no sugars, salt or stabilizers)
1 cup powdered skim milk (non-instant if possible)
1 pound seed mixture (a packaged blend, such as backpacker's mix or your own selection of raisins or currants, sunflower seeds, chopped walnuts, peanuts, raw cashews, and toasted sesame seeds)
¼ cup unfiltered honey or sorghum.

Saran Wrap™ or wax paper

Hot Fudge Sauce

Recipe from Debra Paget
Houston, Texas
A favorite of many friends in Hollywood, California

Melt butter in sauce pan over low heat. Remove from heat, add cocoa and whisk until smooth. Stir in chopped chocolate, sugar, and evaporated milk. Bring to boil over medium heat, stirring all the while. Remove from heat at once and stir in salt. Cook until thickness desired. Cool briefly, then add vanilla. Keeps well in refrigerator.

5 tablespoons unsalted butter
¼ cup cocoa powder
2 squares of unsweetened chocolate, chopped
¾ cup granulated sugar
⅔ cup evaporated milk
pinch of salt
1 teaspoon vanilla extract
pecans (optional)

Small sauce pan

Debra's numerous movie credits include a starring role in Cecil B. De Mille's production of "The Ten Commandments."

Desserts

Chocolate Soufflé

Recipe from Dr. Robert and Arvella Schuller
A favorite of Dr. Robert Schuller
The Crystal Cathedral, Garden Grove , California
Host of <u>Hour</u> <u>of</u> <u>Power</u> seen on TBN

B utter a soufflé dish; sprinkle with sugar. Combine the flour, ¼ cup sugar, salt and milk in a saucepan; blend well. Bring to a boil, stirring constantly. Cook for one minute longer, stirring constantly. Remove from heat. Add chocolate; stir until melted. Stir a small amount of the hot mixture into the beaten egg yolks. Cool. Beat the egg whites and cream of tartar into a bowl until soft peaks form. Add ½ cup sugar gradually, beating until stiff. Fold the chocolate mixture into the egg whites one third at a time. Fold in the vanilla Pour into the prepared soufflé dish. Bake for 30 to 40 minutes or until set. Serve immediately with sweetened whipped cream.

butter
sugar
⅓ cup flour
¼ cup sugar
¼ teaspoon salt
1½ cups milk
three 1-ounce squares
** unsweetened chocolate,**
** crumbled**
6 egg yolks, beaten
6 egg whites
⅛ teaspoon cream of tartar
½ cup sugar
2 teaspoons vanilla extract

Oven Temperature 350°

Saucepan
Soufflé dish
Mixing bowl

Elvis' Favorite Vanilla Ice Cream

Recipe from Dottie Rambo
Gospel Songwriter and Recording Artist
Nashville, Tennessee
A favorite recipe of Elvis Presley

Combine sugar, eggs, butter extract, vanilla, and junket. Pour into ice cream freezer. Fill with milk and cream to four inches from top. Makes one gallon.

2½ cups of sugar
3 small eggs, well beaten
1 tablespoon butter extract
3 tablespoons vanilla
1½ junket, dissolved in warm water
milk
cream

An ice cream freezer

One gallon container

Desserts

Apple Crisp

Recipe from Ruthie Crouch Brown
A favorite of Al Brown, Chief of Staff, TBN
Paul Crouch's Sister and Brother-in-law

Mix together first five ingredients and place in buttered pan. Sprinkle topping over all and bake for 40 to 45 minutes.

4 cups sliced apples
   (in buttered pan)
¾ cup sugar
1 teaspoon cinnamon
½ teaspoon salt
¼ cup water

Topping, mix together:
1 cup flour
1 cup oatmeal
¾ cup brown sugar
½ cup butter

Oven temperature 350°

5" x 7" Baking dish

Buttermilk Pie Cake

Recipe from Mrs. Dave (Brenda) Roever
A favorite of Dave Roever
Host of the <u>Dave</u> <u>Roever</u> program seen on TBN

Melt butter in pan. Combine cake mix and 2 eggs. Pat into pan. Blend cream cheese and 2 eggs. Add powdered sugar and pour over cake. Bake for 30 minutes.

1 box yellow cake mix
4 eggs
1 stick butter
8 ounces cream cheese
1 box powdered sugar

Oven temperature 350°

9" x 13" Pan

Desserts

Creme Bruleé

Recipe from Mrs. Ted (Joyce) Dawson
A favorite of Ted Dawson
Sportscaster
Albuquerque, New Mexico

Combine egg yolks and ½ cup of sugar in the top half of a double boiler, over boiling water. Whisk or beat with a mixer until lemon color, until the consistency of mousse. Remove from heat and set aside. Place cream and vanilla bean in a heavy saucepan. Bring to a boil over medium heat and remove immediately. Strain through a fine sieve. Then pour in egg yolks whisking rapidly as you pour. Return double boiler to heat and cook stirring constantly. cook for 10 minutes or until mixture is quite thick. Remove top half of double boiler and place inside a bowl of ice. Stir occasionally while mixture cools, until it reaches the consistency of a very thick custard. Spread a single layer of fresh raspberries over the bottom of the pastry shells. Pour cooled creme over the raspberries to the top of the pastry shells. Refrigerate for at least 3 hours. When chilled, sprinkle 2 tablespoons of sugar over each shell and place 6 inches from broiler flame for 3 minutes or until sugar crystallizes. Do not over cook or creme will melt. Pour raspberry sauce over bottom of plate and place shell on top of and serve immediately.

6 extra large egg yolks
1½ cups of sugar
3 cups of heavy cream
1 vanilla bean
1 cup of raspberries
6 puff pastry shells
raspberry sauce

Double boiler
Heavy saucepan
Strainer

210

Texas Sheet Cake

Recipe from Mrs. Jim (Connie) McClellan
A favorite of Jim McClellan
Host of JOY seen on TBN and
Manager of Ch. 24, Portland, Oregon
National Minority TV (A TBN Affiliate)

Mix first three ingredients: water, cocoa, and margarine in saucepan and bring to a boil. Set aside. Mix remaining ingredients in a bowl, add hot cocoa mixture, mix well. Pour onto cookie sheet and bake 20 minutes.

Topping:
Bring to boil ½ cup of margarine, 2 tablespoons of cocoa, 3 tablespoons of milk. Add ½ box of powdered sugar, ½ cup chopped walnuts, ½ teaspoon of vanilla. Spread on warm cake.

1 cup of water
4 tablespoons of cocoa
1 cup of margarine
2 cups of flour
½ teaspoon of salt
2 cups of sugar
1 teaspoon soda
½ cup of sour cream
1 teaspoon of vanilla
2 eggs

Oven temperature 350°

Cookie sheet

Desserts

Millie's Fruit Cake

Recipe from Mrs. Bernard (Naomi) Ridings
A favorite of Bernard Ridings
Northland Cathedral, Kansas City, Missouri
Paul Crouch's Sister and Brother-in-law

Put 4 layers of waxed paper in the bottom of 2 bread pans. Mix together the first six ingredients then pour the Eagle™ brand milk over it, mix well and store in the refrigerator overnight. Take out the next morning and put half in each bread pan. Push together firmly and bake for 1 hour. Take out of pans immediately and wrap in waxed paper. It keeps well.

2 cups English walnuts
1 cup pecans
1¾ cup of dates
1½ cup candied cherries
**   (1 pound)**
1 pound candied pineapple
one 14-ounce can coconut
2 cans Eagle™ brand milk

Oven temperature 300°

Wax paper
2 Bread pans
Mixing bowl

Fresh Coconut Cake

Recipe from Mrs. J. Don (Gwen) George
A favorite of J. Don George
Calvary Temple, Irving, Texas

Follow directions on back of Duncan Hines™ white layer cake mix. Bake 2 cakes, cool and slice horizontally. Mix all ingredients together except flake coconut. Stir until sugar dissolves. Frost with icing all 4 layers. Sprinkle with coconut after icing cake. Keep in refrigerator

2 Duncan Hines™ white cake mixes
1 package frozen fresh coconut
2 small cartons fresh sour cream
one 8-ounce Cool Whip™
1 cup sugar
Baker's™ Angel Flake coconut

Two 9" cake pans

Desserts

Mama's Plain Cake

Recipe from Ricky Van Shelton
Country and Gospel Recording Artist
Nashville, Tennessee

Preheat oven to 300°. Grease and flour tube pan. Cream butter and sugar together. Add one egg at a time, beating after each egg. Alternate adding the milk and the flours, beating after each addition until all is mixed well. Add the vanilla and lemon flavoring. Pour in cake pan. Bake for one hour. Let cool.

2 sticks of butter or
    margarine
2½ cups of sugar
4 large eggs
1 cup of milk
1½ cup self-rising flour
1½ cups all purpose flour
1 teaspoon vanilla
1 teaspoon lemon flavoring

Oven temperature 300°

Tube pan

Ricky's latest album is <u>Greatest</u> <u>Hits</u> <u>Plus</u>.

Chocolate Cake

Recipe from Bonnie R. Sheaffer
A favorite of Dr. Daniel T. Sheaffer
Crossroads Cathedral, Oklahoma City, Oklahoma
Hosts of The Answer *seen on TBN*

Bring *Group A* ingredients to a boil, then cool. Mix *Group B* ingredients, add the cooled sauce and beat (batter will be thin). Pour batter into greased and floured 13" x 9" pan and bake for 20 minutes at 400°.

Icing:
Bring cocoa, milk, and margarine to a boil and add powdered sugar, vanilla and pecans or coconut. Pour icing over the cake when it is first removed from the oven (while it's still hot). Serves 8 (we're big eaters!).

Group A:
4 tablespoons cocoa
1 stick margarine
½ cup Crisco™
1 cup water

Group B:
2 cups sugar
2 cups flour
1 teaspoon baking soda
½ teaspoon salt
1 cup buttermilk
2 eggs

For Icing:
4 tablespoons cocoa
6 tablespoons milk
1 stick margarine
1 pound box powdered sugar
1 teaspoon vanilla
1 cup pecans or coconut

Oven temperature 400°

13" x 9" Greased and floured pan

Buttermilk Pie Cake

Recipe from Mrs. Dave (Brenda) Roever
A favorite of Dave Roever
Host of the Dave Roever program seen on TBN

Melt butter in pan. Combine cake mix and 2 eggs. Pat into pan. Blend cream cheese and 2 eggs. Add powdered sugar and pour over cake. Bake for 30 minutes.

1 box yellow cake mix
4 eggs
1 stick butter
8 ounces cream cheese
1 box powdered sugar

Oven temperature 350°

9" x 13" Pan

Apple Cake

Recipe from Dom DeLuise
Actor/Comedian
Los Angeles, California

In mixing bowl cream butter, sugar, and egg. Stir together dry ingredients, add to creamed mixture (batter will be very thick). Stir in the apples, nuts, and vanilla, spread into greased baking pan. Bake for 35 to 40 minutes or until cake tests done. Serve warm or cold with whipped cream or ice cream.

**3 tablespoons of butter
softened**
1 cup of sugar
1 egg beaten
1 cup of flour
½ teaspoon of cinnamon
½ teaspoon of salt
1 teaspoon of baking soda
3 cups of peeled apples
¼ cup of chopped nuts
1 teaspoon of vanilla extract
1 tablespoon of lemon rind

Oven temperature 300°

8" Square baking pan

Desserts

Poppy Seed Cake

Recipe from Mrs. Mylon (Ann) LeFevre
Contemporary Gospel Recording Artist
Marietta, Georgia

Mix all ingredients. Grease bundt pan (I use PAM™), then sprinkle with sugar. Pour into pan then bake 40 minutes.

1 box of Duncan Hines™ batter with pudding cake mix
8 ounces of sour cream
⅓ cup of sugar
4 eggs
¾ cup of Wesson™ oil
2 ounces of poppy seed

Oven temperature 350°

Bundt pan

Mylon's latest album is <u>Mylon</u> <u>LeFevre</u> <u>&</u> <u>Friends</u>.

Mrs. B.'s Coconut Cake

Recipe of Laurie Leard Bethany
Jan Crouch's Mother

Cream shortening, add sugar and beat well. Add eggs, one at a time, beating after each one. Alternate milk and flour that has been sifted with baking soda. Add vanilla. Bake in three layers. They will be thin. Cook about 25 minutes. Make your own recipe of white mountain icing. Ice between each layer and on top. Use three packages of fresh frozen coconut between layers and on top and sides of cake. Moist and delicious, wonderful to serve at holiday time. Serves approximately 10 to 12.

2 cups flour
2 cups sugar
4 eggs
1 cup buttermilk or
 1 carton yogurt
½ teaspoon baking soda
1 teaspoon vanilla
1 cup shortening (soft)
3 packages fresh frozen
 coconut

3 Cake pans, greased and
 floured

Desserts

Carrot Cake with Buttermilk Glaze

Recipe from Ella Smith
A favorite of Pastor Ed Smith
Trinity Christian Center of
Santa Ana, California

Sift together flour, soda, cinnamon and salt; Set aside. Beat eggs in bowl until lemon colored; beat in sugar, oil, buttermilk, and vanilla. Stir in pineapple, carrots, nuts, coconut and flour mixture. Pour batter into lightly greased and floured baking pan. Bake for 55 to 60 minutes, until cake tests done.

Frosting:
Combine all ingredients (except vanilla) in saucepan; bring to boil. Boil 5 to 6 minutes, until thick and syrupy; add vanilla. Poke holes in top of cake with wooden pick or fork; pour glaze over top of cake while cake is still hot. Serve warm or store in refrigerator.

2 cups all-purpose flour
2 teaspoons baking soda
2 teaspoons cinnamon
½ teaspoon salt
3 eggs
2 cups sugar
¾ cup vegetable oil
¾ cup buttermilk
2 teaspoons vanilla
1 can (8¼ ounces) crushed
    pineapple, well drained
2 cups very finely grated
    carrots
1 cup chopped walnuts
1 cup flaked coconut

Buttermilk glaze:
1 cup sugar
½ cup buttermilk
½ cup butter
1 tablespoon white corn syrup
½ teaspoon baking soda
1 teaspoon vanilla

Oven temperature 350°

13" x 9" Baking pan
Saucepan

Desserts

Ultimate Carrot Cake

Recipe from Reba Rambo McGuire
A favorite of Dony and Reba Rambo McGuire
Contemporary Gospel Songwriters and Recording Artists
Nashville, Tennessee

Combine first six ingredients, then set aside. Next, combine sugars, buttermilk, oil, eggs and vanilla in large mixing bowl; stir until well blended. Slowly add flour mixture, carrots and remaining ingredients, stirring until well blended. Grease the three pans; then line the bottom of the pans with wax paper. Grease and flour on top of the wax paper. Pour even amounts of the batter into cake pans. Bake for 30 minutes or until wooden pick inserted in center comes out clean. Cool in pans for 10 minutes. Loosen cake layers from edge of pan with sharp knife. Invert on wire racks, then peel off wax paper. Let cool.

Cream cheese frosting:
Combine butter and cream cheese in large mixing bowl, beat until light and fluffy. Add remaining ingredients and beat until fluffy. Refrigerate cake before serving.

Dony and Reba's latest album is
<u>Suddenly</u>.

1½ cups of whole wheat flour
⅔ cups of all purpose flour
2 teaspoons baking soda
2 teaspoons ground cinnamon
½ teaspoon ground nutmeg
⅛ teaspoon ginger
1 cup of sugar
1 cup of firmly packed brown sugar
1 cup of buttermilk
¾ cups of vegetable oil
4 eggs
1½ teaspoons of vanilla
1¼ pounds grated carrots
one 8-ounce can of crushed pineapple (drained)
1 cup of chopped walnuts
1 cup of flaked coconut
1 cup of raisins

Cream cheese frosting:
½ cup of butter or margarine, softened
one 8-ounce cream cheese, softened
one 16-ounce box of powdered sugar
1 teaspoon of vanilla extract

Oven temperature 350°

Three 8" round cake pans
Large mixing bowl

221

Desserts

Chocolate Chip Cheesecake

Recipe from Karen Kelley
Gospel Recording Artist
Glendale, California

Mix butter and crushed Oreos™ together lining bottom of pan, set aside. Beat cheese until fluffy, then add milk. Beat until smooth. Add eggs and vanilla, mix well. Coat ½ cup of chips with flour, then stir into batter. Put in spring form pan. Sprinkle remaining chips over all batter. Bake for one hour until cake springs back to the touch.

¼ cup of melted butter
1½ cup crushed Oreos™
(about 18 cookies
with filling)
three 8-ounce packages of
cream cheese , softened
14 ounces of sweetened
condensed milk
1 cup of mini chocolate chips
1 teaspoon of flour
3 eggs
2 teaspoons of vanilla

Oven temperature 300°

9" spring form pan

Karen's latest album is <u>The</u> <u>Desire</u> <u>Of</u> <u>My</u> <u>Heart</u>.

Paul Jr. and Matt's Favorite Birthday Cake

Recipe from Jan Crouch
Hosts of <u>Praise</u> <u>the</u> <u>Lord</u> seen on TBN
A favorite of Paul Jr.and Matt Crouch

Slice angel food cake into 2 or 3 horizontal layers. Place one layer of cake on a serving dish and pile on ½" softened chocolate ice cream, then smash all the peanut M&M™ candies you can squash into the ice cream. Repeat between layers 2 and 3. Freeze immediately and serve in slices.

1 large bakery angel food cake
½ gallon chocolate ice cream (softened)
1 large bag peanut M&M™ candies

Cake serving dish

"A beautiful, wonderful, colorful, fun cake for birthdays that you'll love because you have the ice cream, cake and candies all in one slice!" –Jan

Desserts

Chocolate Chip Date Cake

Recipe from Mrs. Jack (Anna) Hayford
A favorite of Pastor Jack Hayford
Church on the Way, Van Nuys, California
Host of Living Way seen on TBN

Pour 1½ cup boiling water over 1 cup chopped dates with 1 teaspoon baking soda and ½ cup shortening. Let cool. Mix 2 eggs (beaten), 1 cup sugar, 1¼ cup flour plus 3 tablespoons, ¼ teaspoon salt, ¾ teaspoon baking soda. Add date mixture. Pour into greased and floured pan. Sprinkle chocolate chips over top of batter and ½ cup sugar and ½ cup nuts (if desired). Serve with whipped cream or vanilla ice cream.

1½ cups boiling water
1 cup chopped dates
baking soda
1½ cup shortening
2 eggs (beaten)
sugar
1¼ cup plus
    3 tablespoons flour
¼ teaspoon salt
1 small package chocolate
    chips
chopped nuts (if desired)
whipped cream or
    vanilla ice cream

Oven Temperature 350°

13" x 9" Pan

Wacky Chocolate Cake

Recipe from Sister R.W. Schambach
A favorite of Dr. R. W. Schambach
Host of Voice of Power seen on TBN

Combine all ingredients in mixing bowl (don't sift flour). Mix until smooth. Bake for about 45 minutes.

3 cups flour
2 cups sugar
¾ cup cocoa
2 teaspoons baking soda
½ teaspoon salt
1 cup oil (canola)
2 cups water
2 teaspoons vanilla extract

Oven temperature 350°

Two 9" cake pans
Large mixing bowl

Desserts

Piña Colada Cake

Recipe from Vonette Bright
A favorite of Dr. Bill Bright
Campus Crusade for Christ
Host of New Life 2000 seen on TBN

Prepare cake as directed on box. Bake in 9" x 13" pan. When it comes out hot from the oven, poke holes in cake, 1" apart. The more holes you poke, the more liquid it will absorb. Pour condensed milk over entire cake. Let cool. Pour Piña Colada mix over top. Spread Cool Whip™ and then sprinkle coconut all over the cake. Serve right away or refrigerate overnight. Serves 12 to 16.

1 yellow cake mix
1 can Eagle™ brand
    condensed milk
1 cup Piña Colada mix
one 8-ounce container of
    Cool Whip™
1 can flake coconut

9" x 13" pan

Mississippi Mud Cake with Icing

Recipe from Pat Brock
A favorite of Steve Brock
Gospel Recording Artist
Host of the <u>Steve Brock</u> program seen on TBN

Cream sugar and shortening; add eggs, and beat by hand. Sift flour, cocoa, and salt. Add to above mixture. Mix, then add vanilla and nuts. Pour into greased and floured oblong pan, bake 35 minutes at 300°. Take out of oven and pour marshmallows over top. Put back in oven for 10 minutes at 350°. Cool cake 1 hour.

Icing:

Sift sugar and cocoa. Mix with melted margarine; add cream and vanilla. Add nuts, and spread on cake. Cake serves 24.

2 cups sugar
1 cup shortening
4 eggs
1½ cups flour
⅓ cup cocoa
3 teaspoons vanilla
1 cup chopped nuts
½ teaspoon salt
½ of 10½-ounce package of
    miniature marshmallows

Icing:

2 sticks margarine
⅓ cup cocoa
1 box powdered sugar
¼ to ⅓ cup canned milk or
    cream
1 teaspoon vanilla
1 cup nuts

Oven temperature 300°

*Teflon coated aluminum sheet
    cake pan*

Steve's latest album is <u>Going Up With A Shout</u>.

Desserts

Betty Mills'
Triple Chocolate Cake

Recipe from Betty Mills
A favorite of Walt Mills
Gospel Recording Artist
Host of <u>Revival</u> <u>In</u> <u>The</u> <u>Land</u> seen on TBN

Combine first six ingredients and mix until smooth with electric mixer. Fold in chocolate chips. Bake for 55 minutes. Cool in pan for a few minutes, turn out on plate. Cool.

Chocolate icing:
Combine ½ cup melted butter, ½ cup cocoa, about ¾ pound powdered sugar, cream or milk to thin to spreading consistency.

Optional:
Shave chocolate on top.

1 Duncan Hines™ Swiss Chocolate Mix
1 large package instant chocolate pudding
4 eggs
½ cup warm water
1/2 cup vegetable oil
1 cup sour cream
one 12-ounce package chocolate chips

Chocolate icing:
½ cup melted butter
½ cup cocoa
¾ pound powdered sugar
cream or milk for thinning

Oven temperature 350°

Tube pan (well greased)

Walt's latest album is <u>Hotel</u> <u>Hallelu</u>.

228

Desserts

Baker's™ German Chocolate Cake and Coconut Pecan Frosting

Recipe from Jan Crouch
A favorite of Paul Crouch
Founders and President of TBN
Hosts of Praise the Lord *seen on TBN*

Lavishly rich, lusciously moist, unlike any other cake. This luxurious cake can be made only with creamy, light Baker's™ German Sweet Chocolate. Melt 1 package Baker's™ German Sweet Chocolate in ½ cup boiling water. Cool. Cream 1 cup butter or margarine and 2 cups sugar until light and fluffy. Add 4 egg yolks, one at a time, beating after each. Add 1 teaspoon vanilla and melted chocolate. Mix until blended. Sift together: 2½ cups sifted flour, 1 teaspoon baking soda, ½ teaspoon salt. Add flour mixture to the chocolate alternately with 1 cup buttermilk, beating after each addition until smooth. Fold in 4 egg whites, stiffly beaten. Pour batter into three 9" layer pans, lined on bottoms with paper. Bake in moderate oven (350°) for 30 to 35 minutes. Cool. Add frosting.

Coconut Pecan Frosting:
Combine in saucepan: Cook over medium heat, stirring constantly until thickened, about 12 minutes. Remove from heat. Add about 1⅓ cups Baker's™ Angel Flake coconut and 1 cup chopped pecans. Beat until cool and of spreading consistency. Make 2⅔ cups, or enough for tops of three 9" layers.

1 package Baker's™ German Sweet Chocolate
1 cup butter or margarine
2 cups sugar
4 eggs
1 teaspoon vanilla
2½ cups sifted flour
1 teaspoon baking soda
½ teaspoon salt
1 cup buttermilk

Coconut Pecan Frosting:
1⅓ cups Baker's™ Angel Flake coconut
1 cup chopped pecans
1 cup evaporated milk
1 cup sugar
3 egg yolks
¼ pound butter or margarine
1 teaspoon vanilla.

Oven temperature 350°

Saucepan
Three 9" layer pans, lined on bottoms with paper

"A German cake for this ol' German!"

229

Desserts

Coca-Cola™ Cake

Recipe from Mrs. Rick (Cindy) Godwin
A favorite of the Rick Godwin family
Eagle's Nest Christian Fellowship, San Antonio, Texas
Host of Reaching Higher seen on TBN

Combine sugar and flour. Heat butter, cocoa, Coca-Cola™ to a boiling point. Pour over sugar and flour mixture. Beat well. Add buttermilk, eggs, baking soda and vanilla. Beat well. Add marshmallows (they will be floating on the top). Pour into greased and floured 9" x 13" pan. Bake at 350° for 35 minutes. Ice cake while hot with icing.

For Icing:
Heat butter, cocoa, Coca-Cola™ to boiling point. Pour over powdered sugar. Beat well until smooth. Add nuts and vanilla, mix well. Pour over cake while hot. Cake serves 12 to 15.

2 cups sugar
2 cups flour
2 sticks butter
1 cup Coca-Cola™
3 tablespoons cocoa
½ cup buttermilk
2 beaten eggs
1 teaspoon vanilla
1½ cup miniature
    marshmallows
1 teaspoon baking soda

For Icing:
½ cup butter
3 tablespoons cocoa
6 tablespoons Coca-Cola™
1 box powdered sugar
1 cup chopped nuts
1 teaspoon vanilla

Oven temperature 350°

9" x 13" Pan

Cheese Cake

Recipe from Mrs. Esther Shelton (not pictured)
(Rexella Van Impe's Mother)
A favorite of Dr Jack and Rexella Van Impe
Hosts of <u>Jack Van Impe Presents</u> seen on TBN

Crush graham crackers and mix with ½ pound of butter, two tablespoons of sugar and pinch of cinnamon. Press into the bottom and along the sides of a 9" round baking dish. (Save 2 tablespoons of crushed graham crackers to sprinkle on top of cake.). Mix cake ingredients and pour over graham cracker crust. Bake at 350° for 20 minutes and cool at room temperature for one hour. Mix topping ingredients and pour over cream cheese mixture. Bake again at 350° for 5 minutes, sprinkle with graham cracker crumbs, cool to room temperature and refrigerate.

For Cake:
¾ pound of cream cheese, softened
one 20-ounce can of crushed pineapple, well-drained
2 eggs, unbeaten
½ cup of sugar
½ teaspoon of vanilla

For Crust:
12 graham crackers
½ pound of butter
2 tablespoons of sugar
a pinch of cinnamon

For Topping:
1 pint of sour cream
3 tablespoons of sugar
1 teaspoon of vanilla

Oven temperature 350°

9" Round baking dish

Desserts

Miss Kittie's Orange Frosting

Recipe from Kathy Hayes
A favorite of Mike and Kathy Hayes
Covenant Church, Carrollton, Texas

Mix cream cheese and butter until well blended and fluffy. Thoroughly mix in powdered sugar, vanilla, orange liqueur (or orange flavoring) and orange peel. Add walnuts and raisins and stir until blended.

one 8-ounce cream cheese (room temperature)
1½ cup or 1 stick of butter (room temperature)
½ teaspoon vanilla
1 tablespoon orange flavored liqueur or orange flavoring
1 tablespoon orange peel grated fine
½ cup chopped walnuts or pecans
½ cup golden raisins

Lemon Icebox Meringue Pie

Recipe from Pat Avanzini
A favorite of Dr. John Avanzini
Host of Biblical Economics seen on TBN

Combine milk, egg yolks and lemon juice into deep medium size bowl and mix until filling is thick. Pour into graham cracker pie crust. Whip egg whites until they make peaks, add sugar gradually and continue to whip until peaks are firm. Cover pie filling with meringue. Place in oven at 350° until meringue is golden brown. Cover and refrigerate until ready to serve.

graham cracker pie crust
1 can Eagle™ brand
    condensed milk
2 eggs
½ cup lemon juice
3 tablespoons sugar

Oven temperature 350°

Medium size bowl

Desserts

Southern Pecan Pie

Recipe from Mary Brown
A favorite of Dean and Mary Brown
Gospel Songwriter and Recording Artists
Hosts of Music That Ministers *seen on TBN*

B eat eggs, add corn syrup, butter and vanilla; blend well. Combine sugar and flour; add to egg mixture. Add chopped pecans. Pour into pie shell, bake 40 to 50 minutes for 9" shell, or 25 to 30 minutes for tarts, until filling is firm. This pie is more flavorful served the next day!

one 9" unbaked pie shell
   (I prefer 15 to 16
   tart shells)
3 whole eggs, well beaten
1 cup light corn syrup
1 tablespoon melted butter or
   margarine
1 teaspoon vanilla extract
1 cup chopped pecans
1 cup granulated sugar
1 tablespoon flour

Oven temperature 350 to 375°

9" pie pan or cookie sheet
*   for tart shells.*

"My parents in Arkansas have lots of pecan trees, so if you were a guest in our home, this would be one dessert, for sure, that I would serve." –Mary

Dean and Mary's latest album is I Am Determined.

Papa Quinn's Pecan Pie

Recipe from Z. W. Quinn (not pictured)
(Charles Quinn's Father)
A favorite of Charles and Laurie "Ditty" Quinn
Trinity Agapé Church, Hallandale, Florida
Jan Crouch's Sister and Brother-in-law

Cream butter. Combine eggs, syrup, milk and vanilla. Then combine sugar, salt, flour, and pecans. Mix all ingredients together thoroughly and pour into unbaked pie shell. Top with pecans, chopped. Bake in moderate oven 40 to 50 minutes or until set. Very delicious, a family favorite! Serves 6.

½ cup butter
2 eggs
1 cup light corn syrup
½ cup milk
½ teaspoon vanilla
½ cup light brown sugar
¼ teaspoon salt
1 tablespoon flour
1 cup chopped pecans
unbaked pie shell

Oven temperature 350°

Desserts

Pecan Pie

Recipe from Dodie Osteen
A favorite of John and Dodie Osteen
Lakewood Church, Houston, Texas

Melt margarine. Add sugar, Karo™ syrup and eggs. Beat well. Add vanilla and pecans. Pour in unbaked pie shell. Bake 30 to 40 minutes, until firm in middle.

Variations:
For three pies at once, add 5 eggs to above recipe and triple other ingredients.

Coconut Pie:
Leave off pecans. Add 1 cup coconut.

French Lemon Pie:
Leave off pecans. Add 2 tablespoons flour and ¼ cup lemon juice.

¾ **cup Karo™ syrup**
¾ **cup sugar**
3 eggs
⅓ **stick margarine**
1 teaspoon vanilla
1 cup pecans
   (chopped or whole)
1 Unbaked pie shell in pie pan

Oven temperature 350°

English Apple Pie

Recipe from Peggy McMillan
A favorite of Terry McMillan
Gospel Recording Artist and Harmonica Player
Nashville, Tennessee

In medium bowl beat oleo and brown sugar until fluffy. Stir in flour, 1 teaspoon cinnamon, and water until smooth and thick. Stir in pecans. Mix sugar with 2nd teaspoon of cinnamon. Mound apples in baking dish sprinkle sugar and cinnamon over apples. Spoon pecan batter over apples in dollops. Bake 45 to 50 minutes.

½ **cup oleo**
½ **cup packed brown sugar**
1 **cup all purpose flour**
2 **teaspoons cinnamon**
3 **tablespoons water**
½ **cup chopped pecans**
4 **large apples peeled, cored, and sliced**
½ **cup sugar**

Oven temperature 375°

Square Pyrex™ baking dish
Mixing bowl

Desserts

Betty Price's Cheese Pie

Recipe from Mrs. Frederick K.C. (Betty) Price
A favorite of Dr. Frederick K.C. Price
Crenshaw Christian Center, Los Angeles, California
Host of Ever Increasing Faith seen on TBN

Mix together (may appear a little lumpy) and put into pie crust. Cook for 20 minutes at 350°. Remove from oven and sprinkle cinnamon all over pie. Cook another 5 minutes

For Topping:

Cover entire pie with topping and put back in oven for 10 minutes. Cool to room temperature and put in refrigerator overnight.

For Pie Filling:
two 8-ounce packages cream cheese, room temperature
⅔ cup sugar
2 eggs
½ teaspoon each almond and vanilla flavoring
cinnamon
one graham cracker crust.

For Topping:
½ pint sour cream
2 tablespoons sugar
¼ teaspoon each almond and vanilla flavoring

Oven temperature 350°

Bon Bon's Pineapple Delight

Recipe from Bonnie R. Sheaffer
A favorite of Dr. Daniel T. Sheaffer
Crossroads Cathedral, Oklahoma City, Oklahoma
Hosts of The Answer seen on TBN

Crush graham crackers* and mix with sugar and butter. Pat into bottom of 8" x 8" pan and chill.

Layer 2:
Whip Dream Whip™, add sugar and cream cheese. Spread over chilled crust.

Pineapple Topping:
Bring all ingredients to a rolling boil and boil for 1 minute, stirring constantly. Chill and spread over *Layer 2*. Serves 6.

Layer 1:
25 graham crackers
¼ cup sugar
1 stick butter

Layer 2:
1 large package cream cheese
1 cup confectioner's sugar
Dream Whip™

Pineapple Topping:
½ cup sugar
3 tablespoons cornstarch
   (sometimes more)
½ teaspoon salt
¾ cup pineapple juice
1 cup crushed pineapple, well
   drained
1 tablespoon butter
1 teaspoon lemon juice

8" x 8" pan

*To crush the graham crackers, I used to put them in double plastic baggies and set them under the back wheel of the car. After Dan left for the church office, they would be perfect!

Desserts

Sensational Double Layer Pumpkin Pie

Recipe from Dotti Casoria
A favorite of John and Dotti Casoria
Bethany Christian Center, Loganville, Georgia
Jan Crouch's Sister and Brother-in-law

Mix cream cheese, 1 tablespoon milk and sugar in large bowl with wire whisk, until smooth. Gently stir in whipped topping. Spread on bottom of graham cracker pie crust. Pour 1 cup milk into bowl. Add pudding mix. Beat with wire whisk until well blended, 1 to 2 minutes. Mixture will be thick. Stir in pumpkin, add spices with wire whisk; mix well. Spread over cream cheese layer. Refrigerate at least 3 hours. Garnish with additional whipped topping and walnuts, if desired. Serves 8.

4 ounces Philadelphia™ cream cheese, softened (microwave on HIGH 15 to 20 seconds)
1 tablespoon milk or half-and-half
1 tablespoon sugar
1½ cups Cool Whip™ whipped topping, thawed
1 graham cracker pie crust
1 cup cold milk or half-and-half
2 packages (4-serving size) Jell-O™ vanilla flavor instant pudding and pie filling
1 can (16 ounces) pumpkin
1 teaspoon ground cinnamon
½ teaspoon ground ginger
¼ teaspoon ground cloves

Large mixing bowl

Black Bottom Pie

Recipe from Mr. and Mrs. Billy Walker
A favorite of Billy Walker
Country Gospel Singer and Recording Artist
Hendersonville, Tennessee

Soften gelatin in water. Mix ¼ cup sugar and cornstarch together. Add beaten egg yolks and stir in milk. Cook slowly until thickened, stirring constantly. Remove from heat and reserve one cup of the mixture. Add gelatin to remaining mixture and stir until dissolved. Melt one square chocolate and add to reserved mixture. Add 1 teaspoon of vanilla and beat with rotary beater. Cool. Pour into pastry shell and chill. Beat egg whites until frothy, add cream of tartar and beat until stiff; beat in remaining sugar. When gelatin mixture is thickened slightly, fold in egg whites and remaining vanilla. Pour into pastry shell covering chocolate layers. Chill thoroughly. Cover with whipped cream and top with ½ square of grated chocolate.

1 envelope of gelatin
4 tablespoons cold water
½ cup of sugar
1¼ tablespoon cornstarch
2 cups milk scalded
1 baked pastry shell deep dish
½ teaspoon cream of tartar
2 teaspoon vanilla
1 square bitter chocolate

Sauce pan
Rotary beater

Desserts

Creamy Banana Pudding

Recipe from Dotti Casoria
A favorite of John and Dotti Casoria
Bethany Christian Center, Loganville, Georgia
Jan Crouch's Sister and Brother-in-law

In large bowl, combine sweetened condensed milk and water. Add pudding mix, beat well. Chill 5 minutes. Fold in whipped cream. Spoon 1 cup pudding mixture into 2½-quart glass serving bowl. Top with one third each of the wafers, bananas and pudding. Repeat, layering twice, ending with pudding. Chill. Garnish as desired. Refrigerate leftovers.

Tip:
Mixture can be layered in individual serving dishes. Makes 8 to 10 servings.

one 14-ounce can Eagle™ brand sweetened condensed milk (not evaporated milk)
1½ cups cold water
one 4-serving size package instant vanilla flavor pudding mix
2 cups (1 pint) whipping cream, whipped
36 vanilla wafers
3 medium bananas, sliced and dipped in lemon juice from concentrate and drained

2½-Quart glass serving bowl

Banana Cream Pudding

Recipe from Zonelle Thompson
A favorite of Dwight Thompson
Host of the <u>Dwight</u> <u>Thompson</u> program seen on TBN

B lend sugar, cornstarch and salt in saucepan. Combine milk, egg yolks and gradually stir into sugar mixture. Cook over medium to low heat, stirring constantly, until mixture thickens and boils. Remove from heat. Stir in butter and vanilla. Place vanilla wafers on bottom of dish, sliced bananas, pudding. Repeat wafers, bananas, pudding. Top with real whipping cream. Yummy!

½ **cup sugar**
2 **tablespoons cornstarch**
⅛ **teaspoon salt**
2 **cups milk**
2 **egg yolks**
2 **tablespoons butter**
2 **teaspoons vanilla**
bananas
vanilla wafers

Desserts

Bread Pudding

Recipe from Beau and Elvina Williams
A favorite of Beau Williams
Gospel Recording Artist
Arlington, Texas

Place bread on a cookie sheet and toast lightly (preheat oven) about 4 minutes a side, so it won't be too soggy. Break bread into small pieces and place in a bowl. Add all ingredients and drained raisins. Pour mixture into a well-greased 11" x 14" baking dish and bake 20 minutes. The custard should be very slightly browned, but not dry. Serve with lemon sauce. Serves 8 to 12.

12 slices day-old bread
4 eggs, lightly beaten
1½ cups whole milk
1 cup evaporated milk
½ cup sugar
1 teaspoon baking powder
⅓ cup butter, melted
½ teaspoon cinnamon
½ teaspoon nutmeg
⅛ teaspoon ground cloves
3 tablespoons raisins, soaked
  in warm water

Oven temperature 350°

Cookie sheet
11" x 14" Baking dish

Beau's latest album is <u>Love</u>.

244

Rice Pudding

Recipe from Rose Shakarian
A favorite of Demos and Rose Shakarian
Full Gospel Businessmen's Fellowship International
Costa Mesa, California

Beat eggs, sugar, vanilla and milk together. Pour into buttered baking pan and add rice (add small box of raisins, if desired). Sprinkle cinnamon on top and bake for 1 hour. Serves 4.

4 eggs
1 cup of sugar
1 teaspoon vanilla
4½ cups of milk
½ cup of rice
cinnamon

Oven temperature 350°

Desserts

Grandma's Pumpkin Nut Cookies

Recipe from Mrs. Rob (Tammi) Tripp
A favorite of the LaVerne Tripp family
Gospel Songwriters and Recording Artists
Hosts of The LaVerne Tripp Family program seen on TBN

Cream butter until light and fluffy, adding sugar gradually. Add eggs and pumpkin; mix well. Sift flour, baking powder, salt and spices in separate bowl. Stir dry ingredients into wet mixture until blended. Add nuts, stir well. Drop on greased cookie sheet and bake 15 minutes.

½ cup butter
1 cup sugar
2 eggs, beaten
1 cup solid-packed pumpkin
2 cups sifted flour
4 teaspoons baking powder
1 teaspoon salt
2½ teaspoons cinnamon
½ teaspoon nutmeg
¼ teaspoon ginger
1 cup chopped walnuts

Oven temperature 350°

The Tripp's latest album is I'm Still Dancin'.

Special Oatmeal Cookies

Recipe from Naomi Ridings
A favorite of Bernard Ridings and their grandchildren
Northland Cathedral, Kansas City, Missouri
Paul Crouch's Sister and Brother-in-law

Melt the butter in an iron frying pan. Add the oats and brown lightly over medium heat, 3 to 4 minutes, stirring continuously. Remove from heat and add carefully the flour, baking powder and salt. Then add the egg, vanilla and nuts. Drop from a teaspoon on an oiled cookie sheet. Bake for 6 to 8 minutes. Remove to waxed paper while still hot.

¼ **pound real butter (1 stick)**
1 cup old fashioned oats
½ **cup plus 2 teaspoons sugar**
¼ **cup cake flour**
½ **teaspoon baking powder**
½ **teaspoon salt**
1 egg, beaten
½ **teaspoon vanilla**
½ **cup nuts ground**

Oven temperature 325°

An iron frying pan is best to mix these in.
Cookie sheet

Desserts

Deluxe Chocolate Marshmallow Bars

Recipe from Mrs. Scotty (Lucille) Scotvold
A favorite of Scotty Scotvold
Winterhaven, California

In a mixing bowl, cream butter and sugar. Add eggs and vanilla, beat until fluffy. Add flour, baking powder, salt, and cocoa. Add to creamed mixture. Stir in nuts if desired. Spread in greased pan. Bake at 350° 15 to 20 minutes. Sprinkle marshmallows evenly over cake. Return to oven for 2 to 3 minutes. Using a knife dipped in water spread marshmallows evenly over cake. Let cool.

Topping:
Combine chocolate chips, butter, and peanut butter in small saucepan. Cook over low heat, stirring constantly until melted and well mixed. Remove from heat, stir in cereal. Spread over bars and chill.

¾ cup of butter or margarine
1½ cups of sugar
3 eggs
1 teaspoon of vanilla
1⅓ cups of all purpose flour
½ teaspoon of baking powder
½ teaspoon of salt
3 tablespoons of baking cocoa
½ cup of chopped nuts (optional)
4 cups of miniature marshmallows

Topping:
1⅓ cups of chocolate chips (8 ounces)
3 tablespoons of butter
1 cup of peanut butter
2 cups of Rice Crispies™ cereal

Oven temperature 350°

Greased jelly roll pan
Small saucepan for topping

Twenty years ago, God spoke to this precious Lutheran brother, Scotty Scotvold, just in the nick of time to hand-deliver the check that kept us from losing Ch. 40 and ultimately the network. Read the whole story in chapter 14 of I Had No Father But GOD, by Paul F. Crouch, Sr.

Luscious Lemon Squares

Recipe from Mrs. Vern (Sandra) Jackson
A favorite of Vern Jackson
Gospel Recording Artist
Santa Ana, California

Preheat the oven to 350°. In a medium bowl, stir together 2 cups flour and ¼ cup plus 2 tablespoons confectioner's sugar. Cut the margarine into the mixture until it is crumbly. Pat the dough into a 15" x 10" non-stick baking pan. Bake the crust until set, 10 to 15 minutes. In a medium bowl, beat the eggs with the remaining ¼ cup flour, the baking powder, granulated sugar, orange juice concentrate, lemon juice, lemon zest, and vanilla. Pour the egg mixture over the hot crust and bake until the top is set, 12 to 15 minutes. Cool, then sprinkle with the remaining 2 tablespoons confectioner's sugar and cut into 48 squares.

2¼ cups all-purpose flour
½ cup confectioners' sugar
1 cup reduced-calorie unsalted tub margarine
4 eggs
½ teaspoon baking powder
½ cup granulated sugar
½ cup frozen orange juice concentrate, thawed
¼ cup fresh lemon juice
1 tablespoon plus 1 teaspoon grated lemon zest
½ teaspoon vanilla extract

Oven temperature 350°

Medium size bowl
15" x 10" Non-stick baking pan

Vern's real favorite is a Burrito Supreme with green sauce from Taco Bell™ but they wouldn't give him the recipe!

Vern's latest albums are <u>Higher Than I've Ever Been</u>, <u>O Holy Night</u>, and <u>Hello Mama</u>.

Blonde Brownies

Recipe from Mrs. Pat (Shirley) Boone
A favorite of the Pat Boone family
Host of <u>Gospel America</u> seen on TBN

Cream butter and sugar; add egg and vanilla. Sift together dry ingredients; add to sugar and egg mixture gradually. Add nuts; spread into greased pan and sprinkle chocolate ships over top. Bake for 25 to 30 minutes. Cool, cut into squares.

⅓ **cup butter or shortening, melted**
1 **cup brown sugar**
1 **egg, slightly beaten**
1 **teaspoon vanilla**
1 **cup flour**
½ **teaspoon baking powder**
⅛ **teaspoon baking soda**
½ **cup chopped nuts**
½ **package chocolate chips**

Oven temperature 350°

Pat's latest Gospel Music Video is "Israel, O Blessed Israel."

Breakfast

Breakfast

Breakfast Casserole

Recipe from Reeni Fenholt
A favorite of Jeff Fenholt
Contemporary Gospel Recording Artist
Hosts of Highway to Heaven seen on TBN

B utter bottom of pan. Cube 8 slices of bread and line the bottom of the pan. Brown the Jimmy Dean hot sausage and break it up into pieces. Place the sausage pieces over the bread cubes. Beat 6 to 8 eggs. Mix eggs with ½ cup milk and 2½ teaspoons of dry mustard. Pour the egg mixture over the bread and sausage and refrigerate overnight. In the morning, mix 1 can of mushroom soup and ½ cup of milk and pour over sausage mixture. Top with grated cheddar. Bake at 300° for 1 hour. Watch closely after 45 minutes. Some ovens may take longer.

Butter
8 slices bread, cubed
1 Jimmy Dean™ hot sausage
6 to 8 eggs, beaten
½ cup milk
2½ teaspoons of dry mustard
1 can mushroom soup
    (I use cream of
    mushroom)
½ cup milk
grated cheddar

Oven temperature 300°

15" x 9" Baking dish

Jeff's latest album is Jesus 50's.

Love Waffles

Recipe from Mrs. Pat (Dede) Robertson
A favorite of Dr. Pat Robertson
Host of the 700 Club seen on TBN

Heat the waffle iron. Iron is ready when a drop of water forms a small ball. If water sizzles, iron is too hot. Mix ingredients together with a few swift strokes, make like muffin batter. Beat egg whites until they are stiff, not dry. Fold egg whites into batter until they are barely blended. Bake on waffle iron until done. These are very good served with maple syrup, orange syrup, strawberry preserves or fresh fruit. If you have sour milk or sour cream, use 2 eggs instead of 3, and then use 1½ teaspoon baking powder and ¼ teaspoon baking soda. Makes 6 waffles.

1 cup unbleached flour
or ¾ cup flour and ¼ cup
wheat germ
1 cup soybeans
2 teaspoons baking powder
½ teaspoon salt
1 teaspoon sugar
3 egg yolks, beaten
5 teaspoons salad oil or melted
butter
1½ cups milk

Waffle iron
Mixing bowl

Health Breakfast on the Run

Recipe from Judy Lindberg McFarland
A favorite of the McFarland family
Nutritionist
Torrance, California

Put into a blender all the ingredients. If you need a sweetener add a tablespoon of frozen orange juice concentrate or frozen apple juice concentrate (both great natural sweeteners).

6 ounces certified raw (if available) low-fat milk
1 tablespoon soy lecithin
2 heaping tablespoons protein powder or powdered skim milk
½ teaspoon vanilla to taste, optional
½ ripe frozen banana, or other fresh fruit
ice cubes, if no frozen fruit

Blender

Breakfast

Non-Fat Yogurt

Recipe from Judy Lindberg McFarland
A favorite of the McFarland family
Nutritionist
Torrance, California

Heat 1 quart of fresh skim milk. Heat carefully until it is hot, but do not boil. (This is important). Into this hot, but not boiling milk, stir 1 cup of powdered skim milk, plus 3 tablespoons of ready made yogurt. Pour this mixture into a wide mouth thermos jar, cover and let it stand overnight. It takes 4 to 6 hours for yogurt to become solid. The next morning, remove the top of the thermos and place the yogurt in refrigerator.

1 quart fresh skim milk
1 cup powdered skim milk
3 tablespoons ready made
   yogurt

Saucepan
Wide mouth thermos jar

Babushka's Joke Recipes For KIDS Only!

Babushka's Joke Recipes For KIDS Only!

Caylan Crouch and
Babushka

❦ *There's a new restaurant where we can all eat dirt cheap. But who wants to eat dirt?*

❦ *What kind of filling do you want me to put in your tooth? My preference is chocolate fudge!*

❦ *Why did the orange stop in the middle of the expressway? It ran out of juice.*

❦ *What do you get when you cross saltines with a duck? Quackers.*

❦ *What do you call someone who breaks into a butcher's shop? A hamburglar.*

❦ *How can you tell if an elephant is in the refrigerator? The door won't shut.*

❦ *What did the beaver say to the tree? Nice knawing you.*

❦ *When are cooks said to be very cruel? When they beat the eggs and whip the cream.*

❦ *What does a geometry teacher like to eat? A square meal.*

❦ *What book contains more stirring pages than any other book? A cookbook.*

❦ *What is the difference between a tuna fish and a piano? You can't tune a fish.*

❦ *Where would you send a man with a great big appetite? To Hungary.*

❦ Disgruntled diner: *Waiter, the food here is terrible. I won't eat it! You had better get the manager.* Waiter: *Won't do any good. He won't eat here either.*

Finger Paints

Recipe from Brandon, Brittany, and Carra Crouch
Children of Tawny and Paul Crouch, Jr.
Grandchildren of Paul and Jan Crouch

Mix the sugar and cornstarch then add the water. Cook over heat, stirring constantly until well blended. Divide the mixture into 4 to 5 jars and add a different food color to each. Add a pinch of detergent for easy clean-up.

3 tablespoons sugar
½ cup cornstarch
2 cups cold water
food coloring
liquid detergent

Saucepan
4 to 5 Small jars

Dirt Cake

Recipe from Brandon, Brittany, and Carra Crouch
Children of Tawny and Paul Crouch, Jr.
Grandchildren of Paul and Jan Crouch

Crush cookies until fine in a food processor or blender. Set aside. Combine pudding and milk, fold in whipped topping, set aside. Mix cream cheese, butter and powdered sugar. Combine with pudding mixture. Layer pudding and cookie mixture (parfait style) in lined flower pot. Decorate with gummy worms and silk flowers.

20-ounce package Oreo™ cookies
2 small packages instant vanilla pudding
16-ounce non-dairy whipped topping
one 8-ounce cream cheese
1 cup butter
1 cup powdered sugar
gummy worms

Clean flower pot lined with foil
Silk flowers to plant

Silly Putty

Recipe from Brandon, Brittany, and Carra Crouch
Children of Tawny and Paul Crouch, Jr.
Grandchildren of Paul and Jan Crouch

Mix 2 parts glue to 1 part liquid starch. Let dry a bit so that it becomes workable. You can add a few drops of food coloring to give the putty some color. Store in an airtight container.

white glue (If you use Elmer's™ school glue instead of regular white glue, it won't bounce or pick up pictures.)
Sta-Flo™ liquid starch
food coloring

Air tight container

For KIDS Only!

Elephant Stew

Recipe from Mrs. Jess (Doris Cummins) Moody
Shepherd of the Hills Church, Porter Ranch, California
Dr. Moody hosts the <u>Jess Moody</u> program seen on TBN

Cut elephant into 1 inch cubes. This will take about 2 months. Cut vegetables into cubes (another 2 months). Place meat in pan and cover with 1,000 gallons of brown gravy and cook over large gas stove for 4 weeks. Frequently shovel in generous amounts of the salt and pepper. When meat is tender, add vegetables with your rented steam shovel. Simmer slowly 4 more weeks (three if you like your vegetables crispy). Garnish with parsley. Recipe will serve 3,874. But if more are expected for dinner, add the 2 rabbits. This isn't recommended as very few people like hare in their stew!

1 medium elephant
1 ton salt
1 ton pepper
500 bushels potatoes
200 bushels carrots
4,000 sprigs parsley
2 small rabbits

Borrow a big, big pan from
* the space administration*
Rent a steam shovel
Very large kerosene gas stove

A favorite of Patrick and Martha Moody when they were children

Bubble Solution

Recipe from Tawny Crouch
A fun favorite of the Paul Crouch, Jr. family
Paul and Jan Crouch's Son and Daughter-in-law and
Grandchildren – Brandon, Brittany and Carra

Combine and pour into a container. Use a plastic straw or pipe cleaner to make your own designs to blow.

⅓ **cup dish soap or baby**
  shampoo
1½ **cups water**
2 **teaspoon sugar**
1 **drop food coloring**

Plastic container

Goop

Recipe from Tawny Crouch
A fun favorite of the Paul Crouch, Jr. family
Paul and Jan Crouch's Son and Daughter-in-law and
Grandchildren – Brandon, Brittany and Carra

Mix cornstarch and water together. Add paint or food coloring for different colors. Pour into tray or tub to play in.

½ cup cornstarch
½ cup water
tempera paint or
**   food coloring**

Tray or tub

Kool-Aid™ Clay

Recipe from Brandon, Brittany, and Carra Crouch
Children of Tawny and Paul Crouch, Jr.
Grandchildren of Paul and Jan Crouch

Mix together dry ingredients. Add water and oil, mix thoroughly. Let cool, and store in an airtight container.

2 packages unsweetened
   Kool-Aid™
1 tablespoon cream of tartar
½ cup salt
2½ cups flour
2 cups boiling water
3 tablespoons oil

Saucepan
Mixing bowl

Index

Index

Index